The Analects of Confucius

TRANSLATIONS FROM THE ASIAN CLASSICS

Analects of Confucius, stone stele fragment. Imperial scholars, using a special style of calligraphy called *li*, inscribed the Analects and other classical texts on stone stele, which they erected in the Imperial Academy in A.D. 175. The stones were destroyed soon after during the wars that brought the dynasty to an end, and the fragments were buried for protection. They were later unearthed during the Song dynasty. This fragment depicts a section of the *Analects* and measures 52 by 35 centimeters.

The Analects of Confucius

TRANSLATED BY BURTON WATSON

COLUMBIA UNIVERSITY PRESS   NEW YORK

COLUMBIA UNIVERSITY PRESS

Publishers Since 1893
New York   Chichester, West Sussex

Copyright © 2007 Columbia University Press
Paperback edition, 2010
All rights reserved

Library of Congress Cataloging-in-Publication Data

Confucius.
[Lun yü. English]
The Analects of Confucius / translated by Burton Watson.
p. cm.—(Translations from the Asian classics)
Includes bibliographical references.
ISBN 978-0-231-14164-2 (cloth : alk. paper)
ISBN 978-0-231-14165-9 (pbk. : alk. paper)
ISBN 978-0-231-51199-5 (electronic)
I. Watson, Burton, 1925– II. Title. III. Series.

PL2478.L3 2007
181'.112—DC22
2007005401

∞

Columbia University Press books are printed on
permanent and durable acid-free paper.

Printed in the United States of America

C 10 9 8 7 6 5 4 3 2 1
P 10 9 8 7 6 5 4 3

Contents

The Analects of Confucius

Introduction

Lunyu, or *The Analects of Confucius*, has probably exercised a greater influence on the history and culture of the Chinese people than any other work in the Chinese language. Not only has it shaped the thought and customs of China over many centuries, but it has played a key role in the development of other countries that were within the Chinese cultural sphere, such as Korea, Japan, and, later, Vietnam.

Readers encountering the text for the first time might wonder how this rather brief collection of aphorisms and historical anecdotes could have been so influential. The text, probably compiled in stages some time during the fourth century B.C.E., was at first only one of many philosophical works that embodied the teachings of this or that school of early Chinese thought. The followers of the teachings of Confucius were referred to collectively as the *Ru* school, which denotes persons who devote themselves to learning and the peaceful arts (as opposed to martial matters).

Some centuries later, when Emperor Wu (r. 141–87 B.C.E.) of the Han dynasty declared Confucianism the official doctrine of the state, the *Analects* and other texts associated with Confucius assumed enormous importance. They were regarded as repositories of knowledge of how the empire had been governed in the model eras of antiquity and how the Chinese government system, and society as a whole, should be ordered. In still later centuries, the *Analects* was treated as a beginning text in the study of classical Chinese, to be committed to memory and, when students were more advanced, studied exhaustively and with its lessons examined in depth.

CONFUCIUS

According to tradition, Confucius was born in 551 B.C.E. His family name was Kong; his personal name, Qiu; and his polite name (the name by which most persons would have addressed him), Zhongni. The name Confucius is a Latinized form of Kong fuzi, or Respected Master Kong, a title commonly used to refer to him in Chinese.

Confucius was born in the small feudal state of Lu, situated in northeastern China in the area of present-day Shandong Province. His father, who was a member of the *shi* class, the lowest rank of the nobility, died when Confucius was very young. It is clear from the *Analects* that Confucius grew up in considerable poverty, an experience that seems to have made him particularly sensitive to matters of wealth and class. At an early age, as he tells us, he devoted himself to learning, and the importance of education is a major theme in the *Analects*.

The extent to which this "learning" related to written texts and to which it was based on oral traditions is unclear. The *Analects* refers frequently to two texts, the *Book of Odes* and the *Book of Documents*, both of which Confucius, according to legend, had some hand in editing. A third early text, the *Book of Changes*, is mentioned in one version of the *Analects*. These constitute three of what later became known as the five Confucian Classics, the other two being the *Spring and Autumn Annals*, a chronicle of the state of Lu said to have been edited by Confucius, and the *Book of Rites*, a collection of texts on ritual.

Whether Confucius's learning derived from written texts or from oral traditions, he appears to have been intensely concerned with those that reflected the early culture of China, particularly that of the sage rulers Yao and Shun of high antiquity and of the early rulers of the Xia, Yin, and Zhou, the so-called Three Dynasties, when China was believed to have enjoyed exemplary eras of peace and social order. He was especially interested, it would seem, in the rites, music, and other cultural elements that distinguished these periods.

Confucius's ambition, it would appear, was to gain official position in his native state of Lu so that he could put his ideals on morality and good government into practice. Later legend depicts him as, in fact, holding fairly high public office in Lu, but there is little or no evidence in the *Analects* to support such a supposition. To understand the problems that Confucius faced in his search for office, we must review the social and political situation in the China of his time.

The Zhou people, founders of the dynasty under which Confucius lived, came originally from a region in western China. Kings Wen and Wu, who founded the dynasty, probably around 1040 B.C.E., had their capital in the area of present-day Xi'an. Under their rule and that of their immediate successors, China was divided into a vast number of feudal domains whose leaders acknowledged fealty to the Zhou king (or Son of Heaven) and aided him in repelling the attacks of non-Chinese peoples living on China's borders. One such attack in 771 B.C.E., however, forced the Zhou rulers to abandon their original capital in the west and move east to the area of Luoyang, a step that marked the beginning of the era known as Eastern Zhou (771–256 B.C.E.).

By this time, the Zhou kings had ceased to wield any real authority but were allowed to continue occupying the throne because of their religious significance as heads of the ruling clan. Actual power had meanwhile passed into the hands of the rulers of the larger feudal states, such as Qi on the Shandong Peninsula and Jin in northeastern China. In the *Analects*, Confucius is depicted as speaking favorably of the leaders of these two states because of their ability, at least for a time, to restore order and unity to the nation and protect it from foreign invasion.

Because the Zhou kings were no longer strong enough to enforce conditions of order and stability, as they supposedly had in earlier centuries, the more powerful feudal states were able to swallow up their weaker neighbors and ally themselves with one another to advance their aims. Thus the era was marked by almost constant warfare, the feudal lords, who lived in walled cities, venturing forth in

cumbersome war chariots to attack this or that foe, accompanied by foot soldiers enlisted from the peasantry, who ran alongside the chariots. Confucius himself disclaimed any knowledge of military matters and deplored the warlike tenor of the age, but it is reflected in numerous passages of the *Analects*.

In addition to the threat of incursion from predatory neighbors, many of the feudal domains of the time were troubled by succession disputes. Although the principle of primogeniture was recognized in general, rulers at times disregarded it or delayed making clear their choice of an heir. Sons of the ruler, often by different mothers, vied for favor or fled or were exiled from the state entirely, taking up residence in neighboring states where they could gather supporters and, in time, attempt to enforce their claim to rulership. Such a situation is reflected in the *Analects* in the power struggle that ensued after the death of Duke Ling of the state of Wei between his son Kuai Kui and his grandson Che, a struggle in which one of Confucius's leading disciples, Zilu, was killed in combat.

The ruling family of Confucius's native state of Lu traced its descent to Dan, the duke of Zhou, a younger brother of King Wu, the founder of the Zhou dynasty. It was thus of ancient and distinguished lineage, and Confucius looked on the duke of Zhou with particular awe and veneration. But by Confucius's time, the dukes of Lu had lost much of their actual power and authority. As had happened or was in the process of happening in other states, power had passed into the hands of ministerial families—in Lu, three cadet families descended from sons of Duke Huan of Lu and referred to in the *Analects* as the "three Ji families." Powerful ministerial families such as these at times posed a serious threat to the rulers of the feudal domains and, in some cases, eventually overthrew and replaced them or brought about the partitioning of the states.

These, then, were the political conditions that confronted Confucius while he was growing up in Lu and acquiring the knowledge of Chinese history, culture, and ritual practice that allowed him to

become a distinguished teacher. Because of such knowledge and his status as a member of the lower aristocracy, he was permitted to take part in rituals of the ruler's court and, judging from the *Analects*, was at times consulted by the ruler on matters of government. But, as stated earlier, it is doubtful that he ever held a government post of any distinction.

Meanwhile, he gathered around him a number of disciples, some of whom held posts in the service of the Ji families, and these he endeavored to imbue with his standards of moral conduct and political ideals. Failing to gain a hearing from the dukes of Lu, in his middle years he journeyed, together with some of his disciples, to nearby states in the hope of finding a more sympathetic reception for his ideas. But such wanderings proved for the most part disappointing and, at times, even exposed him and his followers to hardship and hostility.

His political ambitions unrealized, Confucius returned to Lu and devoted his remaining years to teaching. According to legend, in these later years he gave himself to the editing and transmission of the five so-called Confucian Classics, though in fact it is uncertain whether some of these texts were even in existence at this time.

According to the *Analects*, he had a daughter, whose marriage he arranged, and a son, Boyu, who died some years before his father. Confucius is said to have died in 479 B.C.E. In *Analects* 14:40, one contemporary of his, clearly not very favorably disposed toward him, describes him as "the one who knows there's nothing that can be done but keeps on trying." That may have been the general assessment of Confucius and his teaching at the time of his death.

THE *ANALECTS*

Lunyu means "Conversations," but the book is customarily referred to in English by the term *Analects*, which refers to a selection from the writings or sayings of a particular person—in this case, Confucius. It consists of a large number of brief passages, some only a sentence

or two in length, arranged in twenty sections, or "Books." There appears to be little or no logic to the arrangement of the material. Many of the passages record sayings attributed to Confucius, "the Master"; others report the words of his disciples or describe historical incidents in which he or his followers figure, while a few passages seem to have little or no connection with Confucius at all.

Understanding of the work is made difficult by the fact that it is among the earliest extended prose works in Chinese and one that attempts to represent the conversational style of the period. It makes frequent use of parallelisms and the carefully balanced style typical of ancient Chinese and often cites rhymed "sayings" or lines of poetry to emphasize a point. At the same time, it employs a variety of particles that lend a conversational tone to the utterances.

It was probably a hundred years or more after the death of Confucius before the *Analects* assumed anything like its present form. Linguistic studies of the text and considerations of content suggest that some parts are of later date than others and that the text represents an amalgam of views held by different groups among the followers of the Confucian school. Readers interested in learning more about these theories regarding the dating of the different sections of the *Analects* may consult works such as E. Bruce Brooks and A. Taeko Brooks's *The Original Analects*. But for those encountering the text for the first time, it is best to read it as a unified whole and in its present order, which is how it has traditionally been read and understood over the centuries in China and the other countries within the Chinese cultural sphere.

The Chinese have shown a marked fondness for pithy sayings and the belief that the most important truths can best be expressed, or at least conveniently summed up, in aphoristic form, a conviction that clearly permeates the wording of the *Analects*. Moreover, they have believed, as evidenced by their abiding concern with the keeping and study of historical records, that ideas are best understood and remembered in the form of events tied to actual historical times and person-

ages. In the *Analects*, therefore, the reader will find no lengthy discussions of terminology or expositions of ideas. Instead, moral and political concepts are presented in terms of particular individuals, the teacher Confucius and the disciple or other person with whom he is conversing, and the particular circumstances under discussion. And because the participants and circumstances vary in different passages, the manner in which the ideas are conveyed varies accordingly. The reader of the *Analects* should be prepared to encounter not a formal treatise but conversations that seek to illuminate or grapple with important concepts, sometimes in clear and succinct form, at other times in more oblique fashion, colored by the sort of surprise, misunderstanding, pleased reaction, displeased reaction, humor, or sarcasm that characterize conversations in real life. The *Analects* endeavors to present insights into the actual exchange of ideas between teacher and student, the activity that was at the core of Confucius's life and importance as an individual.

THE CONFUCIAN TEACHINGS

The best way to approach an overall discussion of the Confucian teachings as they are reflected in the *Analects* may be to examine some of the key terms that Confucius and his disciples employ in their pronouncements.

As stated earlier, we are not certain which texts and oral traditions were available to these persons to provide them with an understanding of early Chinese history. Confucius several times speaks of Yao and Shun, ideal sovereigns who were believed to have ruled the empire in very ancient times. Although the *Analects* makes no clear reference to the fact, Yao was traditionally believed to have passed over his own son and chosen Shun, a man of great virtue but unrelated to him by blood, as his successor. And Shun in time did likewise, it was said, ceding the throne to Yu, because of his moral worth, rather than to his own son. This "ceding" principle, the belief that wisdom and

moral stature rather than birth alone are what qualify one for rulership, seems to underlie much of Confucius's thinking in the *Analects*.
Nowhere does he actually advocate such acts of ceding or openly challenge the idea of hereditary rule. But in discussing the ruler's ministers, he makes clear that, in his view, it is moral standing rather than
birth that qualifies one for official position; he stresses that in matters
of education there should be no class distinctions; and he indicates
that as a teacher he is ready to give instruction to anyone, regardless
of the person's social background, who sincerely desires to learn.

According to legend, Shun's successor, Yu, the founder of the Xia
dynasty, encouraged agriculture, carried out flood-control measures,
and ensured peace and stability within the realm. His reign, and those
of his immediate successors, like those of Yao and Shun, were models
of good government. But in time, the virtue of the Xia rulers declined
until the throne passed to Jie, an evil tyrant. At that point, at least
according to later belief, Heaven (a term discussed later) withdrew
its support, the so-called Mandate of Heaven, from the dynasty and
bestowed it elsewhere. A virtuous leader, King Tang, arose to over-
throw the Xia regime and found a new dynasty, the Shang or Yin,
and once again China enjoyed wise and benevolent rule. The virtue
of the new dynasty, however, followed the same pattern of decline,
ending in the reign of another tyrant, Zhou (written with a different
character from the name of the dynasty that supplanted him). Claim-
ing that they were acting on the Mandate of Heaven, a new group of
leaders emerged to challenge the Yin's rule: King Wen, the Cultured
King, who began the undertaking, and his son King Wu, the Martial
King, who overthrew the Yin, established a new dynasty, the Zhou,
and initiated a new era of peace and upright government.

In the *Analects*, Confucius frequently employs the term *dao*, which
means "a path or way" and, by extension, "a method of doing things."
In some contexts, such as the writings of the Daoist school, the word
has more metaphysical connotations. But in Confucius's pronouncements, it refers specifically to the characteristics of peaceful, benevo-

lent, and culturally distinguished government typical of the periods of ideal rule, particularly that of the early years of the Zhou dynasty.

In the translation that follows, the word *dao* has usually been rendered as "the Way," with a capital "W" to signal its importance. Confucius gives various instructions on how to behave when "the Way prevails in the world" or when it does not. He clearly believed that it did not prevail in his time, as evidenced by the wars, usurpations of power, and departures from correct ritual practice that marked the age. But he also makes clear that he believes it can be restored at any time. China is not fated to suffer chaos and misrule. The common people are the same as those of the halcyon periods of the past; it is only the rulers who have gone astray. With a return to the principles of correct government, the Way can once more be made to prevail.

The ideal rulers of the past are customarily described as *sheng*, or "sages," a term that occurs at times in the *Analects*. Confucius denied that he himself was a sage or that he had ever encountered a sage, though his compatriots in later centuries would dismiss these disclaimers as mere modesty.

If Confucius has little to say about sages, he spends a great deal of time describing those whom he calls the *junzi*. The word originally meant "lord's child" and referred to offspring of the ruling elite. But Confucius, as we have seen, denied that birth alone entitled one to rulership and reinterpreted the term *junzi* to mean someone whose moral standards and superior understanding entitled him, if not to actual rulership, at least to high official position under a hereditary ruler. Other translators have rendered it as "gentleman," "superior man," or "noble person." I have translated it as "gentleman," with the understanding that the word here refers not to birth or class but to moral stature. That it refers to men and not women is clear from what we know of early Chinese society. Women had no legitimate role in politics and, in fact, make almost no appearance in the *Analects*.

Somewhat similar in meaning in the *Analects* is the term *shi*, mentioned earlier as a designation for the lowest level of the aristocracy.

It is sometimes translated as "knight," since men of this class were permitted to ride in the war chariots and fight alongside the nobles of higher rank. Confucius, however, who belonged to the *shi* class, disclaims any knowledge of military affairs and places all emphasis on cultural and peaceful pursuits. When he uses the term *shi*, it seems to be virtually synonymous with *junzi*. I have translated it as "man of station," once more with the understanding that it refers primarily to moral stature rather than to class distinction alone.

Ancestor worship played a vital role in ancient China, and the *Analects* makes frequent mention of sacrifices and other rites performed for the spirits of the dead, as well as for nature deities of the mountains and rivers. Occasionally we find mention of a higher being or entity known as *tian*, translated here as "Heaven." The word may mean simply "sky" and refer to the impersonal forces of nature. More often, it seems to be a synonym for "fate" or "destiny," at times personalized, as when Confucius in a moment of deep grief exclaims, "Heaven is destroying me!" (11:9). Although Confucius speaks reverently of Heaven and the concept had profound significance for him, he has little to say about religious faith in general. In one famous passage, he advises one of his disciples to "respect the gods and spirits but keep them at a distance" (6:22). In trying to guess what he may have meant by this, one should keep in mind that Confucius's overriding concern was with the political conditions of his time and the degree to which they could be remedied by teaching people to pay stricter attention to moral standards. Rulers of the period, and of later eras in Chinese history as well, were often greatly influenced by religious figures who claimed to be able to put them in contact with the spirit world or teach them the secrets of immortality. Confucius's attitude toward the supernatural was probably not agnostic, as has sometimes been claimed. But, as he said on another occasion, "When you don't yet know how to serve human beings, how can you serve the spirits?" (11:12). He wished first of all that his listeners would keep their attention focused on the ills of society.

As one might expect, the *Analects* abounds in terms designating the various ethical values that Confucius wished to encourage in the persons whom he addresses. Most of these, I hope, will be clear enough in meaning from the English renderings used for them in the translation: "trustworthiness," "courtesy," "respect," "reciprocity," and "loyalty," particularly in the sense of loyalty to another person's best interests. Special attention is given to rites, because it was believed that by performing the actions prescribed by ritual one could summon forth in the mind the emotions and attitudes appropriate to the occasion.

Readers might perhaps be surprised to observe the amount of emphasis on the term *xiao*, or "filial obedience or devotion." But Chinese religion at this time, particularly among the upper classes, revolved mainly around veneration of the family ancestors, expressed through periodic sacrifices to them in an ancestral temple or at a family altar. Moreover, the family was envisioned as the inculcator of moral values in the young: one learned first how to pay proper respect to parents and ancestral spirits and how to live in harmony with siblings and other kin. Only after these patterns of behavior had been mastered in the circle of the family could they be extended to the other members of society.

One moral concept—in some respects the most important one in the *Analects*—poses considerable problems for both the translator and the reader. This is the principle referred to as *ren*. It is written in Chinese with a character consisting of the elements for "person" and "two" and is pronounced the same way as the word for "person," allowing speakers at times to create puns based on this similarity. In order to make such puns understandable, and because I believe it to be the best choice, I have translated the term as "humane" when it is used as an adjective and as "humaneness" when in noun form. Other translators have rendered it variously as "benevolence," "supreme virtue," or "the Good."

Confucius employs the word *ren* frequently in his remarks, without ever clearly defining it. His disciples, puzzled, repeatedly question

him about it, but he appears reluctant to discuss the term at length. Although numerous passages in the *Analects* refer to *ren*, the text at one point states: "The Master seldom spoke about . . . humaneness" (9:11). This seeming anomaly is usually explained as resulting from the fact that, although the disciples were careful to preserve whatever comments the Master made on the subject of humaneness, they were dissatisfied that the sum of such comments was not greater.

At times, Confucius seems to imply that humaneness is quite close at hand, not that difficult to achieve; at other times, he pictures it as the loftiest of ideals and repeatedly denies that this or that person of his own time can be said to have achieved it. Perhaps he saw it as a kind of summation of all the other traits that he believed desirable in human relations, an ideal easily envisioned in the abstract, but all but impossible to achieve. Perhaps he believed that defining it too rigorously would only detract from its validity.

Probably because the *Analects* was compiled over a considerable period and represents the views of several different groups among the followers of the Confucian school, it is not always consistent in its presentation of the teachings. Some passages are of only historical interest; others are obscure in meaning or exasperatingly vague. But because Confucius's thinking centers mainly on questions of politics, education, and human relations, the vast majority of his pronouncements and those of his associates remain of vital interest to readers today. Indeed, the very vagueness of the wording has allowed the text to be reinterpreted or readily adapted to fit the changed circumstances of later ages—for example, by interpreting the term *junzi* to apply to women as well as men. As stated earlier, the *Analects* has in the past exercised a profound influence on the development of the culture of China and that of its immediate neighbors. One cannot hope to understand the history of those cultures without a knowledge of its contents. At the same time, it reflects not only a particular set of ideas that occupied one particular era of the past but an embodiment of sentiments and ideals that are relevant to all of human society. That is

no doubt why the *Analects* has retained its validity for more than two thousand years and will continue to do so for the foreseeable future.

A NOTE ON THE TEXT AND INTERPRETATION

There are two main versions of the *Analects*: the Lu and Ku texts. They do not differ greatly, but I have noted in my translation one place where there is an important difference. The exact numbering of the individual passages differs slightly in different editions, and my own numbering may therefore not always coincide with that of other translations.

Commentaries fall into two groups: those dating from the Han and Six Dynasties periods, and later ones by Song dynasty Neo-Confucian scholars. My translation for the most part follows the interpretations that have been most commonly accepted over the centuries in China, the *Analects* as most readers in the past have known it. Where interpretations differ markedly and the differences are of significant interest, I have offered more than one translation of a passage.

In my translation, I have tried as much as possible to follow the wording and word order of the Chinese. The language of the translation, however, is in no way intended to reflect the antiquity of the text. It is in the colloquial English that would be used if these conversations took place today.

OTHER TRANSLATIONS OF THE *ANALECTS*

AMES, ROGER T. *The Analects of Confucius: A Philosophical Translation*. New York: Ballantine Books, 1999.

BROOKS, E. BRUCE, AND A. TAEKO BROOKS. *The Original Analects: Sayings of Confucius and His Successors (0479–0249)*. New York: Columbia University Press, 1998.

DAWSON, RAYMOND. *The Analects*. Oxford: Oxford University Press, 1993.

HINTON, DAVID. *The Analects*. Washington, D.C.: Counterpoint, 1998.

LAU, D. C. *The Analects*. Harmondsworth: Penguin, 1979.

LEGGE, JAMES. *The Analects*. Vol. 1 of *The Chinese Classics*. 1861. Reprint, Hong Kong: University of Hong Kong Press, 1960.

POUND, EZRA. *Confucius*. New York: New Directions, 1951.

SLINGERLAND, EDWARD. *Confucius Analects: With Selections from Traditional Commentaries*. Indianapolis: Hackett, 2003.

WALEY, ARTHUR. *The Analects of Confucius*. London: Allen & Unwin, 1938.

In addition to these complete translations, selected translations from the *Analects* are in the following:

BLOOM, IRENE. "Confucius and the *Analects*." In Wm. Theodore de Bary and Irene Bloom, eds., *Sources of Chinese Tradition*, vol. 1, pp. 41–63. 2nd ed. New York: Columbia University Press, 1990.

CHAN, WING-TSIT. "The Humanism of Confucius." In Wing-tsit Chan, trans. and comp., *A Source Book in Chinese Philosophy*, pp. 588–653. Princeton, N.J.: Princeton University Press, 1963.

Book One

1   The Master said, Studying, and from time to time going over what you've learned—that's enjoyable, isn't it? To have a friend come from a long way off—that's a pleasure, isn't it? Others don't understand him, but he doesn't resent it—that's the true gentleman, isn't it?

2   Master You said,[1] A man filial to his parents, a good brother, yet apt to go against his superiors—few are like that! The man who doesn't like to go against his superiors but likes to plot rebellion—no such kind exists! The gentleman operates at the root. When the root is firm, then the Way may proceed. Filial and brotherly conduct—these are the root of humaneness, are they not?

3   The Master said, Clever words and a pleasing countenance—little humaneness there!

4   Master Zeng said, Each day I examine myself on three matters. In making plans for others, am I being loyal to them? In my dealings with friends, am I being trustworthy? Am I passing on to others what I have not carefully thought about myself?

5   The Master said, Guiding a state of a thousand chariots,[2] be attentive to affairs and trustworthy, frugal in expenditures and sparing of others. Employ the common people only at proper times.[3]

6   The Master said, Young people should be filial at home, brotherly with others, circumspect, and trustworthy. Let them act kindly toward the populace in general and befriend those of humane character. If, after that, they have energy left over, let them study the arts.[4]

---

1   For the identity of Master You and other persons mentioned in the text, see the glossary. A few of Confucius's more distinguished disciples are addressed as "Master."
2   The domain of a feudal lord.
3   Call them up for forced labor or military service only when they are not busy with farm work.
4   Literature, rites, music, and so on.

7 Zixia said, If he treats worthy persons as worthy and is respectful to them, does all in his power to serve his father and mother, gives his best in the service of the ruler, and in dealings with friends is faithful to his word, though some may say he lacks learning, I would surely call him learned!

8 The Master said, If the gentleman lacks gravity, he won't command respect. If he studies he will avoid narrow-mindedness. Put prime value on loyalty and trustworthiness, have no friends who are not your equal,[5] and, if you make mistakes, don't be afraid to correct them.

9 Master Zeng said, Tend carefully to death rites, and pay reverence to those long departed, and the people will in the end be rich in virtue.

10 Ziqin questioned Zigong, saying, When the Master goes to a particular state, he is certain to learn about its government. Does he seek such information? Or do others just give it to him?

Zigong said, The Master goes about it by being cordial, forthright, respectful, modest, and deferential. The Master's way of seeking is different from that of others.

11 The Master said, While his father is alive, observe his intentions. After his father is dead, observe his actions. If after three years he hasn't changed his father's way of doing things, then you can call him filial.

12 Master You said, What ritual values most is harmony. The Way of the former kings was truly admirable in this respect. But if in matters great and small one proceeds in this manner, the results may not always be satisfactory. You may understand the ideal of harmony and work for it, but if you do not employ ritual to regulate the proceedings, things will not go well.

13 Master You said, Trustworthiness is close to rightness—it ensures that people will live up to their word. Courtesy is close to ritual

5 That is, in moral character.

decorum—it ensures that people will give wide berth to shame and disgrace. When one makes no mistakes in what he favors, he can serve as a leader.[6]

14 The Master said, A gentleman when he eats doesn't try to stuff himself, when he chooses a dwelling is not overly concerned about comfort. He is attentive to affairs, careful of his words, and looks to those who have the Way to correct himself. He's the kind who can be called a lover of learning.

15 Zigong said, Poor but free of obsequiousness, rich but free of arrogance—how would that do?

The Master said, All right. But not as good as poor but happy in the Way, rich but a lover of rites.

Zigong said, When the *Odes* says:

As something cut, something filed,
something ground, something polished[7]

is that what it's talking about?

The Master said, Si (Zigong), now I can begin to talk to you about the *Odes*. Someone tells you the first step, and you understand the step that comes after!

16 The Master said, Don't worry about whether other people understand you. Worry about whether you understand other people.[8]

---

6 The sentence is obscure and open to widely differing interpretations.
7 *Book of Odes*, no. 55, which describes a man of elegant bearing. Zigong takes the lines to refer to moral training.
8 That is, judge them correctly.

Book Two

1　The Master said, Conduct government in accordance with virtue, and it will be like the North Star standing in its place, with all the other stars paying court to it.

2　The Master said, The three hundred poems of the *Book of Odes* may be summed up in a single phrase: Think nothing base.[1]

3　The Master said, Guide them with government orders, regulate them with penalties, and the people will seek to evade the law and be without shame. Guide them with virtue, regulate them with ritual, and they will have a sense of shame and become upright.

4　The Master said, At fifteen I set my mind on learning; by thirty I had found my footing; at forty I was free of perplexities; by fifty I understood the will of Heaven; by sixty I learned to give ear to others; by seventy I could follow my heart's desires without overstepping the line.

5　Meng Yi Zi asked about filial devotion. The Master replied, Never break the rules.

When Fan Chi was driving the carriage, the Master reported this to him, saying, Meng Sun (Meng Yi Zi) asked me about filial devotion. I told him, Never break the rules.

Fan Chi said, What did you mean by that?

The Master said, While they are alive, serve them according to ritual. When they die, bury them according to ritual, and sacrifice to them in accord with ritual.

6　Meng Wu Bo asked about filial devotion. The Master said, Your father and mother should have to worry only about your falling ill.

1　Quoting a phrase from poem no. 297 and interpreting it out of context, Confucius stresses his view of the didactic import of the *Book of Odes*. In the poem, the words refer to carriage drivers and mean something like "Ah, never swerving!"

[Or, according to another interpretation of the last clause:] In the case of one's father and mother, one just worries about their falling ill.

7   Ziyou asked about filial devotion. The Master said, Nowadays it's taken to mean just seeing that one's parents get enough to eat. But we do that much for dogs or horses as well. If there is no reverence, how is it any different?

8   Zixia asked about filial devotion. The Master said, The difficult part is the facial expression.[2] As for young people taking on the heavy work when there's something to be done, or older people going first when there's wine and food—can this be called filial devotion?

9   The Master said, I talk a whole day with Hui, and he never disagrees with me, as though he were stupid. But later, when I examine his private conduct, I see that it fully exemplifies my ideas. No, Hui is not stupid.

10 The Master said, Watch what he does, observe the path he follows, examine where he comes to rest—can any person then remain a mystery? Can any person remain a mystery?

11 The Master said, Be thoroughly versed in the old, and understand the new—then you can be a teacher.

12 The Master said, The gentleman is not a utensil.[3]

13 Zigong asked about the gentleman. The Master said, First he puts his words into action. Only later does he follow up with explanations.

14 The Master said, The gentleman is fair-minded and not partisan. The petty man is partisan and not fair-minded.

15 The Master said, Learning without thought is pointless. Thought without learning is dangerous.

---

2   Watching the faces of one's parents to make certain how they are reacting Or perhaps the meaning is keeping the proper expression on one's own face.

3   Not something to be used because he has some special knowledge or ability.

16 The Master said, To delve into strange doctrines can bring only harm.[4]

17 The Master said, You (Zilu), shall I teach you what it means to know something? When you know, to know you know. When you don't know, to know you don't know. That's what knowing is.

18 Zizhang was studying to gain an official position. The Master said, Hear much, put aside what's doubtful, and in your speech apply the rest with caution—then you'll make few mistakes. Observe much, put aside what's suspicious, and in your actions apply the rest with caution—then you'll have little to regret. Making few mistakes, having little to regret—the way to official position lies in this.

19 Duke Ai asked, saying, How can I make the common people submissive? Confucius replied, Promote the straight and let them oversee the crooked—then the common people will be submissive. Promote the crooked and let them oversee the straight—then the common people will not be submissive.

20 Ji Kangzi asked, How can I make the common people respectful, loyal, and diligent in their work?

The Master said, If you are strict in overseeing them, they will be respectful. If you are filial and compassionate, they will be loyal. If you promote persons of goodness and teach those who are incompetent, then the people will be diligent.

21 Someone questioned Confucius, saying, Why aren't you in government?

The Master said, The *Book of Documents* says: Filial, only be filial, a friend to elder and younger brothers—this contributes to government.[5] To do this is in fact to take part in government. Why must I be "in government"?

---

4 No one knows just what Confucius means by this. Perhaps the term *yiduan*, translated here as "strange doctrines," has some quite different meaning, though it suggests going off in an unusual direction.

5 From a lost section of the *Book of Documents*.

22 The Master said, Persons who lack trustworthiness—I don't know how they get by! Big carts that have no yoke-bar, little carts that have no collar-bar—how can you go anywhere in them?

23 Zizhang questioned the Master, saying, Can we know how things will be ten generations from now?

The Master said, Yin followed the rites of Xia, and we know in what ways it added to or subtracted from them. Zhou follows the rites of Yin, and we know in what ways it added to or subtracted from them. Whoever carries on from Zhou, we can know how things will be even a hundred generations from now.

24 The Master said, To sacrifice to those who are not one's ancestors is flattery. To see what is right and not do it is cowardly.

Book Three

1 Confucius observed of the Ji family, They have eight rows of dancers in their courtyard. If this can be excused, what cannot be excused?[1]

2 The three Ji families used the Yong ode when the sacrifices were being carried away.[2] The Master said,

> *Assisting are the great lords,*
> *the Son of Heaven in majesty,*

How can this be used in the halls of the three Ji families?

3 The Master said, A human being who lacks humaneness—what is ritual to someone like that? A human being who lacks humaneness—what is music to someone like that?

4 Lin Fang asked what is basic in ritual. The Master said, A big question indeed! In rites in general, rather than extravagance, better frugality. In funeral rites, rather than thoroughness, better real grief.

5 The Master said, The Yi and Di tribes with their rulers cannot match the Xia people without a ruler.[3]

6 The head of the Ji family was planning to make a sacrifice to Mount Tai.[4] The Master said to Ran You, Can't you save him from this?

1 According to Zhou ritual, only the Son of Heaven was privileged to have eight rows of dancers in the ceremonies in the courtyard before his ancestral temple. Persons of lower rank were expected to have a lesser number. The Ji families were ministers to a feudal lord and hence considerably lower in rank, yet they usurped the rites of the supreme ruler. Confucius sees this as an indication of social disharmony and moral decay.

2 *Book of Odes*, no. 282. As the lines quoted by Confucius indicate, it was intended for use in sacrifices at which the Son of Heaven and the great feudal lords were present.

3 The Yi and Di were non-Chinese peoples who lived to the east and northwest of the Chinese, the Xia people.

4 The sacrifice that the head of the Ji family proposes to perform is appropriate only to a feudal lord, not to one of his ministers.

Ran You replied, No, I can't.

The Master said, Are we to suppose that Mount Tai knows less about ritual than Lin Fang?

7 The Master said, The gentleman never strives with others. To be sure, there are the archery matches. But even they have their bows and deferences as the contestants go up and come down, and the wine drinking at the end. Such is the "striving" of the gentleman.

8 Zixia asked, saying,

> *Her artful smile engaging,*
> *lovely eyes in clear outline,*
> *colors on a white ground,*[5]

What do these lines mean?

The Master said, The painting comes after the white background.

Zixia said, So ritual comes afterward?

The Master said, Shang (Zixia) is the one who reads my meaning. At last I have someone to discuss the *Odes* with.

9 The Master said, As for the Xia rites, I could describe them, but the state of Qi can't provide the proofs I need. As for the Yin rites, I could describe them, but the state of Song can't provide the proofs I need.[6] This is due to the lack of records and persons of authority. If these were sufficient, I could prove my words.

10 The Master said, As for all that comes after the libation to the spirits in the ancestral sacrifice—I have no wish to see it.[7]

11 Someone asked about the meaning of the ancestral sacrifice. The Master said, I don't know. Someone who knew its meaning would

5 *Book of Odes,* no. 57. Only the first two lines are found in the present text of the *Odes.*

6 The descendants of the Xia rulers were enfeoffed in the small state of Qi in order to carry on their ancestral sacrifices; those of the Yin rulers, in the state of Song.

7 The *di* sacrifice to the ancestral spirits was ordinarily performed by the Son of Heaven alone. But because of Lu's close connections with the founders of the dynasty, the ruler of Lu had been given special permission to perform it. Evidently, Confucius disapproved of something about the way the ritual was performed

understand all the affairs of the world as if they were displayed right here—and he pointed to his palm.

12 Sacrifice as if they were present means to sacrifice as if the gods were present. But the Master said, If I can't take part in the sacrifices, it's as though I haven't sacrificed at all.

13 Wangsun Jia said,

> *Better pay compliments to the kitchen stove*
> *than to the southwest corner.*[8]

What does this mean?

The Master said, Not true! If you incur blame with Heaven, you have nowhere to turn for forgiveness![9]

14 The Master said, Zhou surveyed the two dynasties that went before, its ways are refined and elegant. I follow Zhou.

15 When the Master entered the Grand Temple,[10] he asked questions about everything. Someone said, Who claims that this son of a man of Zou[11] understands ritual? When he enters the Grand Temple he asks about everything!

When the Master heard this, he said, Asking is part of the ritual.

16 The Master said,

> *In archery hitting the target is not the point—*
> *people are not all of equal strength.*

That was the old-time way.

17 Zigong wanted to do away with the sacrificial sheep at the first-of-the-month announcement to the ancestors. The Master said, Si (Zigong), you care about the sheep; I care about the ritual.

---

8 The southwest corner of the house, where sacrifices to the ancestors were held.
9 A folk saying, meaning that it is better to make sure you have enough to eat rather than worrying about the ancestors. Confucius rejects this cynical view.
10 The ancestral temple of Lu, dedicated to the duke of Zhou, the founder of the state.
11 Birthplace of Confucius's father.

18 The Master said, In serving the ruler, if you carry out all the acts prescribed by ritual, people think you are toadying.

19 Duke Ding asked how the ruler should treat his ministers and how the ministers should serve the ruler.

Confucius replied, The ruler should treat his ministers in accordance with ritual. The ministers should serve the ruler with loyalty.

20 The Master said, The Guanju ode[12]—joy, but not excessive; sadness, but not to the point of injury.

21 Duke Ai asked Zai Wo about the altar to the god of the soil. Zai Wo replied, The Xia rulers planted it with pines, the men of Yin planted it with cedars, and the men of Zhou plant it with chestnuts (*li*), in order, they say, to make the common people tremble (*li*).[13]

When the Master heard of this, he said, Completed affairs one does not comment on; things done one does not carp over; what is past one does not criticize.

22 The Master said, Guan Zhong was a man of small parts!

Someone objected, saying, Guan Zhong was noted for frugality, was he not?

The Master said, Guan Zhong had his Three Returnings mansion,[14] and he did not require his staff to perform double duties—how can that be called frugal?

But, said the other person, Guan Zhong understood ritual, did he not?

---

12 *Book of Odes*, no. 1, which describes a young man pining for his love and the later happy union of the pair.

13 Confucius perhaps did not approve of this pun on *li* (chestnut/tremble) because of its linking of government with feelings of fear.

14 Various explanations of the name Three Returnings are given, one being that it housed Guan Zhong's three wives. In any event, Confucius disapproved of the way Guan Zhong, an official of the state of Qi, imitated the ways of a ruler.

The Master said, Rulers of states put up gate screens, and Mr. Guan put up a gate screen too. Rulers of states, when entertaining another ruler, have a stand for inverted wine cups, and Mr. Guan had a stand for inverted wine cups too. If Mr. Guan understood ritual, who doesn't understand ritual?

23 The Master, speaking with the Grand Music Master of Lu, said, Music can be understood in this way. The players first in unison, then freely harmonizing, playing separately or carrying on from one another, and thus the piece is completed.

24 The border guard of Yi requested an interview with Confucius, saying, When gentlemen pass this way, I never fail to have an interview with them.

The Master's followers arranged a meeting. When the border guard emerged from the interview, he said, You young men should not worry about your present bad luck. For a long time now the world has been without the Way. Heaven is going to use your Master as a wooden-clappered bell.[15]

25 Of the Shao music, the Master said, Perfect in beauty, perfect in goodness. Of the Wu music, he said, Perfect in beauty, but not perfect in goodness.[16]

26 The Master said, Standing above others but without tolerance, carrying out rites but without reverence, conducting funeral proceedings but without grief—how can I bear to view such as these?

---

15 A bell with a wooden clapper, used to summon people for important announcements.
16 The Shao, or "Succession," music was said to date from the time when Shun ascended the throne peacefully ceded to him by Yao. The Wu, or "Martial," music was from the time when the Zhou dynasty forcefully overthrew the Yin. The music was probably accompanied by dance performances.

Book Four

1 The Master said, Humaneness is the beauty of the community. If you can choose but do not make humaneness your home, how can you be called wise?

2 The Master said, A person lacking in humaneness cannot endure straightened circumstances for long, nor can he enjoy favorable circumstances for long. The humane person rests in humaneness, the wise person profits from humaneness.

3 The Master said, Only the humane person is able to like others and is able to hate others.

4 The Master said, Truly set your mind on humaneness, and you will be without evil.

5 The Master said, Wealth and eminence are what people desire, but if one can't get them by means that accord with the Way, one will not accept them. Poverty and low position are what people hate, but if one can't avoid them by means that accord with the Way, one will not reject them.

If the gentleman rejects humaneness, how can he be worthy of the name of gentleman? The gentleman never departs from humaneness even for the space of a meal—in confusion and distress he holds fast to it; stumbling, faltering, he holds fast to it.

6 The Master said, I have never seen a person who really loved humaneness or a person who really hated the lack of humaneness. A person who really loved humaneness would have no one who surpassed him. A person who really hated the lack of humaneness would conduct himself humanely, never allowing those who lack humaneness to affect his behavior.

Is there someone who for a whole day is willing to use all his strength to achieve humaneness? I've never seen anyone who

lacked the strength to do so—there may be such a person, but I've never seen one.[1]

7 The Master said, People's errors vary with the category they belong to. Look at the errors, and you know the degree of humaneness.

8 The Master said, Hear the Way in the morning, and it won't matter if you die that evening.

9 The Master said, A man of station whose will is set on the Way but who is ashamed of poor clothing and poor food—not worth talking to!

10 The Master said, With regard to worldly affairs, the gentleman has no strong likes and no strong dislikes—he sides with what is right.

11 The Master said, The gentleman has his mind fixed on virtue; the petty man has his mind fixed on land. The gentleman has his mind fixed on penalties; the petty man has his mind fixed on bounty.

12 The Master said, Act only with profit in mind, and you face much rancor.

13 The Master said, Can you govern the state with ritual and a deferential approach? Then you will have no difficulty. If you cannot govern the state with ritual and a deferential approach, then what use is ritual alone?

14 The Master said, Don't worry that you have no position[2]—worry about how you can qualify for one. Don't worry that people don't know you—look for some reason to become known.

15 The Master said, Shen (Master Zeng), my Way has one theme running throughout!

Master Zeng said, Yes.

---

1 What we lack is not the strength but the determination to do so.
2 Confucius probably means a position in government, but the saying has much broader implications.

After the Master left, the disciples asked, What did he mean?

Master Zeng said, The Master's Way consists of loyalty and reciprocity[3] alone.

16 The Master said, The gentleman is alert to what is right. The petty man is alert to what is profitable.

17 The Master said, When you see a worthy person, think about how you can equal him. When you see an unworthy person, reflect on your own conduct.

18 The Master said, In serving your father and mother, you may gently admonish them. But if you see they have no intention of listening to you, then be respectful as before and do not disobey them. You might feel distressed but should never feel resentful.

19 The Master said, While his father and mother are alive, a son should not go on distant journeys. If he travels, he must have a fixed destination.

20 The Master said, If after three years [a son] has not changed his father's way of doing things, then you can call him filial.[4]

21 The Master said, You must not be ignorant of the age of your father and mother! For one thing, it is a cause for rejoicing; for another, a cause for fear.

22 The Master said, People in old times were sparing in their words. They were ashamed to think that their actions might not measure up.

23 The Master said, Those who go wrong by holding back are few.

24 The Master said, The gentleman desires to be hesitant in speech but prompt in action.

25 The Master said, Virtue is not alone. It invariably has neighbors.

26 Ziyou said, Be too censorious in serving the ruler, and you will end up in disgrace. Be that way with your friends, and you will lose them.

3 Fellow feeling, doing to others as you would have them do to you.
4 A truncated version of 1:11.

Book Five

1   The Master said of Gongye Chang, He deserves a wife. Although he was bound and imprisoned, he was guilty of no crime.

And he gave him his own daughter for a wife.

2   The Master said of Nan Rong, If the state is ruled by the Way, he will not be overlooked. If the state is not ruled by the Way, he will still stay clear of penalties and punishments.

And he gave him the daughter of his elder brother for a wife.

3   The Master said of Zijian, A real gentleman, this one! If there were no gentlemen in Lu, how could he have become like this?

4   Zigong asked, What would you say of me?

The Master said, You are a vessel.

What kind of vessel? Zigong asked.

A fine sacrificial vessel, said the Master.

5   Someone said of Yong, He is humane but lacking in eloquence.

The Master said, Why does he need to be eloquent? People who overwhelm others with their glibness often end up hated by others. I don't know if Yong is humane, but why does he need to be eloquent?

6   The Master urged Qidiao Kai to take an official position, but he replied, I am not yet confident I'm up to it. The Master was pleased.

7   The Master said, The Way does not go forward—I'll get on a raft and set out to sea! And the one who will go with me will be You (Zilu), will it not?

When Zilu heard this, he was delighted.

The Master said, You outdoes me in love of bravery, though he doesn't always think where that may lead him.

8   Meng Wu Bo questioned Confucius, saying, Is Zilu a humane person?

The Master said, I don't know.

Meng Wu Bo asked again.

The Master said, In a state of a thousand war chariots, You (Zilu) could be put in charge of military levies. But I don't know if he is humane.

What about Qiu (Ran You)?

The Master said, For a town of a thousand households or a clan of a hundred chariots, Qiu could act as overseer. But I don't know if he is humane.

What about Chi (Gongxi Zihua)?

The Master said, Chi, dressed in formal robes, standing in court, would do very well to discourse with the visitors and guests. But I don't know if he is humane.

9   The Master questioned Zigong, saying, Between you and Hui, which is the better man?

Zigong replied, How could I dare hope to equal Hui? Hui hears one part and understands ten. I hear one part and understand two.

The Master said, No, you are not his equal. You and I are neither of us his equal.

10   Zai Yu (Zai Wo) was given to sleeping in the daytime. The Master said, Rotten wood can't be carved; a wall of stinking earth can't be troweled. What's the use of trying to reprimand Yu?

The Master said, At first, when it came to people, I listened to their words and trusted their conduct. Now, when it comes to people, I listen to their words and observe their conduct. It was Yu who brought about this change.

11   The Master said, I have never seen a person of true firmness. Someone said, What about Shen Cheng? The Master said, Cheng is all desires. How can he be called a man of firmness?

12   Zigong said, What I don't want others to do to me, I want to avoid doing to others. The Master said, Si (Zigong), you haven't gotten to that stage yet.

13 Zigong said, The Master's views on cultural and emblematic matters—these we have heard. But his views on human nature and the Way of Heaven—these we have never been able to hear!

14 When Zilu had heard something and had not yet been able to put it into practice, his only fear was that he might hear something else.

15 Zigong asked, Why was Kong Wenzi given the posthumous name Cultured (Wen)?

The Master said, Clear-sighted and a lover of learning, he was not ashamed to ask questions of his inferiors. Therefore he was given the name Cultured.

16 The Master said of Zichan, He exemplified the Way of the gentleman in four respects. In conducting himself, he was prudent. In serving his superiors, he was respectful. In looking out for the common people, he was caring. And in employing the common people, he followed what was right.

17 The Master said, Yan Pingzhong was skilled in his dealings with others. Even toward those he had known for a long time, he remained respectful

18 The Master said, Zang Wenzhong housed a large tortoiseshell for divination in a hall whose pillars were capped with hill-shaped designs and whose joists had a duckweed pattern.[1] What can one think of the wisdom of such a person?

19 Zizhang asked, saying, Ziwen, the prime minister of Chu, served three times as prime minister but showed no sign of delight, and three times was dismissed from the post but showed no sign of resentment. As former prime minister, he invariably reported to the new prime minister on affairs of state. What do you think of this?

The Master said, He acted with loyalty.

Was he humane?

I don't know how he can be called humane.

---

1   The use of a large tortoiseshell for divination and the architectural decorations mentioned were privileges reserved for the ruler of a state.

Cui Zi assassinated the ruler of Qi. Chen Wen Zi, who for his carriages owned ten four-horse teams,[2] abandoned them and left the state. When he arrived in another state, he said, The people here are no better than our high official Cui Zi! and he left that state. Arriving in another state, he said, More like our high official Cui Zi! and he left that state, too. What would you say of him?

The Master said, A man of integrity.

Was he humane?

I don't know how he can be called humane.

20 Ji Wen Zi thought three times before he acted. When the Master heard of this, he said, Twice is enough.

21 The Master said, In the case of Ning Wu Zi, when the Way prevailed in the state, he was wise. When the Way did not prevail in the state, he was stupid. His wisdom can be equaled, but not his stupidity.

22 When the Master was in Chen, he said, Let's go home, let's go home! The young people of our district are in high spirits but hasty. The cloth has been handsomely woven, but no one knows how to cut it.[3]

23 The Master said, Bo Yi and Shu Qi did not dwell on old wrongs— so they had few feelings of rancor.

24 The Master said, Who claims that Weisheng Gao was honest? When someone came to borrow vinegar from him, he borrowed some from a neighbor and then gave it to the person.

25 The Master said, Clever words, a pleasing countenance, politeness overdone—Zuoqiu Ming would be ashamed of such, and I would be ashamed too. To hide your distaste for someone and become that person's friend—Zuoqiu Ming would be ashamed of that, and I would be ashamed too.

---

2 The number of horses Chen Wen Zi owned indicates how eminent he was.

3 That is, the people of Lu, and Confucius's disciples in particular, are ready and eager to be led in the right direction, but they need Confucius to guide them.

26 Once, when Yan Yuan and Zilu were accompanying him, the Master said, Why don't each of you speak of your desires?

Zilu said, I wish that I and my friends could share the same carriages and horses, robes and furs, and never worry if we wore them out.

Yan Yuan said, I would like never to boast of what good points I have and never cause trouble to others.

Zilu said, I would like to hear the Master's desires.

The Master said, To free old people from worry, to be trustworthy toward my friends, and at all times solicitous of the young.

27 The Master said, It's hopeless! I have yet to see anyone who can recognize his faults, look inside himself, and put the blame there.

28 The Master said, In a village of ten households there are certain to be those who are as loyal and trustworthy as I am, but none my equal in love of learning!

Book Six

1   The Master said, Yong (Zhonggong Ran Yong) could be given a seat facing south.[1]

2   Zhonggong asked about Zisang Bozi. The Master said, He will do—he's lenient in nature.

Zhonggong said, If he is strict with himself but lenient when it comes to overseeing the common people, will that be all right? If one is lenient with himself and behaves toward others in a lenient manner, that's too much leniency, isn't it?

The Master said, What you say is correct.

3   Duke Ai questioned Confucius, saying, Who among your disciples loves learning?

Confucius replied, There was Yan Hui—he loved learning, never took his anger out on others, never repeated his mistakes. Regrettably, he had a short life and is dead now. Since then, there are none who love learning, or none I've heard of.

4   Zihua went on a mission to the state of Qi. Ran Qiu asked that Zihua's mother be given an allowance of grain. The Master said, Give her a peck. When Ran Qiu asked for more, the Master said, Give her a bushel. Ran Qiu in the end gave her five large measures of grain.

The Master said, When Chi (Gongxi Zihua) set off for Qi, he had a team of fat horses and was wearing light furs. The way I've heard it, the gentleman helps out the needy but does not contribute to the upkeep of the rich.

5   When Yuan Si was given the post of steward, he was offered an allotment of nine hundred measures of grain, but he declined it.

The Master said, Oh, no! You could have shared it with your neighboring communities, couldn't you?

---

1   The ruler sits facing south.

6 The Master said of Zhonggong, The calf of an ordinary cow, if it is red in color and has proper horns, [is fit to be used as a sacrifice,] though people might hesitate to do so. Surely the gods of the mountains and rivers will not reject it.[2]

7 The Master said, As for Hui, he could go three months without in his mind ever departing from humaneness. The others can do so for a day or a month, but that is all!

8 Ji Kangzi asked, Would Zhongyou (Zilu) be suitable to hold government office?

The Master said, Zhongyou is decisive. Why wouldn't he do for government office?

Would Si (Zigong) do for government office?

The Master said, Si is knowledgeable. Why wouldn't he do for government office?

Would Qiu (Ran Qiu) do for government office?

The Master said, Qiu is talented. Why wouldn't he do for government office?

9 The Ji family wanted to appoint Min Ziqian as steward of Bi. Min Ziqian said, Can someone kindly refuse this offer for me? If they continue to press me, I will have to retire to the banks of the Wen River.[3]

10 Boniu (Ran Boniu) had an illness.[4] The Master went to ask how he was, holding his hand through the window. He said, We are going to lose him. It's fate, is it not? Such a man, and to have such an illness. Such a man, and to have such an illness.

11 The Master said, What a fine man Hui was! One container of rice, one dipperful of drink, living in a back alley—others couldn't have endured the gloom of it, but he never let it affect his happiness. What a fine man Hui was!

2 The implication is that Zhonggong Ran Yong, who was of humble origin, was nevertheless worthy to hold high office.

3 The river that formed the boundary between the states of Lu and Qi.

4 The illness is said to have been leprosy.

12 Ran Qiu said, It's not that I don't delight in the Master's Way, but I don't have sufficient strength for it.

The Master said, Those whose strength is insufficient go at least halfway before giving up. But now you are setting limits for yourself.

13 The Master said to Zixia, You should be a gentleman scholar. Don't be a petty man scholar.⁵

14 Ziyou was made steward of Wucheng. The Master said, Have you come upon any good men?

Ziyou said, There's Tantai Mieming. He doesn't take any short-cuts, and he never comes to my room unless it is on official business.

15 The Master said, Meng Zhifan never boasted. When our forces fled in defeat, he guarded the rear. But when he was about to enter the city gates, he whipped up his horses, saying, I wasn't deliber-ately lagging behind—my horses wouldn't go any faster.⁶

16 The Master said, If you have the good looks of Song Zhao but lack the eloquence of Invocator Tuo, you'll have a hard time es-caping blame in the world today.

17 The Master said, Who can go out of a house without using the door? Why does no one use this Way of mine?

18 The Master said, Where solid qualities outweigh refinement, you have rusticity. Where refinement outweighs solid qualities, you have the clerkly style. Refinement and solid qualities beautifully balanced—then you have the gentleman.

19 The Master said, Human life is a matter of honesty. Live without it, and you'll be lucky to escape with your life.

20 The Master said, To know it is not as good as to approve it. To approve it is not as good as to find joy in it.

5 The word *ru*, translated here as "scholar," designates a man who devotes himself to learning and the peaceful arts, as opposed to the military man.

6 Confucius is speaking of the battle in 484 B.C.E. when invading forces from Qi defeated those of Lu outside the gates of the Lu capital.

21 The Master said, To persons of more than middling capability, you can talk of higher matters. To persons of less than middling capability, you cannot talk of such matters.

22 Fan Chi asked about wisdom. The Master said, Work to lead the people toward what is right. Respect the gods and spirits but keep them at a distance—this can be called wisdom.

When he asked about humaneness, the Master said, Humaneness means tending to difficulties first and leaving benefits for later—this can be called humaneness.

23 The Master said, The wise delight in water; the humane delight in mountains. The wise move; the humane are still. The wise are happy; the humane live long.

24 The Master said, With one change, Qi could measure up to Lu. And with one change, Lu could measure up to the Way.[7]

25 The Master said, A *gu* drinking cup that is not a *gu* drinking cup—what a *gu*, what a *gu*![8]

26 Zai Wo asked, If you were to tell a humane person that there was a humane person in a well, would he go to the rescue?[9]

The Master said, Why would he do that? The gentleman can be made to go somewhere but not to fall into a trap. He can be deceived but not completely hoodwinked.

27 The Master said, If the gentleman acquires broad learning in cultural matters and focuses it through ritual, he is hardly likely to go far astray, is he?

---

7 In Confucius's time, Qi was, of course, much larger and more powerful than Lu, but Confucius is no doubt speaking in cultural terms.

8 Confucius is apparently complaining of instances in which the name does not match the reality.

9 A peculiar question. Commentators suggest emending the second "humane person," to read "someone." Zai Wo is asking how far one is expected to go in pursuit of humaneness.

28 The Master had an audience with Nanzi.[10] Zilu was not pleased. Confucius swore an oath, saying, If I have done anything wrong, may Heaven cast me aside! May Heaven cast me aside!

29 The Master said, The virtue embodied in the doctrine of the Mean[11] is of the highest order. But it has long been rare among people.

30 Zigong said, If someone could spread bounty abroad among the people and rescue the populace, how would that be? Could that be called humaneness?

The Master said, Why bring humaneness into the discussion? If you must have a label, call the man a sage. Even Yao and Shun had trouble doing that much.

The humane person wants standing, and so he helps others to gain standing. He wants achievement, and so he helps others to achieve. To know how to proceed on the analogy of what is close at hand—this can be called the humane approach.

10 The wife of Duke Ling of Wei, notorious for her adulterous conduct, which is why Zilu disapproved of the meeting.
11 *Zhongyong*, or "the doctrine of moderation," an important concept in Confucian thought. But it is mentioned only this once in the *Analects*.

Book Seven

1   The Master said, A transmitter and not a maker, trusting in and loving antiquity, I venture to compare myself with our Old Peng.

2   The Master said, To be silent and understand, to learn without tiring, never to weary of teaching others—this much I can do.

3   The Master said, Virtue not sufficiently practiced, learning not sufficiently digested, to hear what is right and not be able to do it, to have shortcomings and not be able to remedy them—these are the things that I worry about.

4   The Master when he was at leisure—very relaxed, very genial.

5   The Master said, How great is my decline! It's been so long since I dreamed that I saw the duke of Zhou!

6   The Master said, Set your sights on the Way, base yourself on virtue, rely on humaneness, relax with the arts.

7   The Master said, If a person comes with a bundle of dried meat or better, I've never refused him instruction.[1]

8   The Master said, If they're not eager to learn, I don't enlighten them; if they're not struggling to put it into words, I don't assist them. I hold up one corner to show them, and if they can't come back with the other three, then I don't go on.

9   When the Master was eating at the side of a person in mourning, he never ate his fill. On a day when the Master had wept for someone, he never sang.

10 The Master said to Yan Yuan, When needed, to act; when cast aside, to retire—only you and I know how to do that—isn't that so?

    Zilu said, If you, Master, were directing the Three Armies,[2] who would you take with you?

---

1   The bundle of dried meat was the student's gift for the teacher, his tuition fee.
2   The armies of a large state.

The Master said, Someone who faces a tiger bare-handed or wades the Yellow River, going to his death with no regrets—I wouldn't take anyone like that. If I must answer, then I'd take someone who directs affairs in a mood of apprehension, who plans carefully and thereby succeeds.

11 The Master said, If one could get rich just by trying, then although it meant being a herald with whip in hand, I would go along with that. But if one can't get rich just by trying, I prefer to follow my own desires.

12 The Master exercised great care with regard to the following: preparations for a sacrifice, warfare, and illness.

13 When the Master was in Qi, he heard the Shao music[3] and for three months no longer knew what sort of meat he was eating. He said, I never supposed that music could reach such heights!

14 Ran You said, Will our Master side with the ruler of Wei?[4] Zigong said, Very well, I'll go and ask him.

Entering the Master's room, Zigong said, What sort of men were Bo Yi and Shu Qi?

The Master said, Worthy men of antiquity.

Did they harbor rancor?

They sought to behave humanely, and they succeeded in doing so. Why would they harbor rancor?

When Zigong emerged from the room, he said, Our Master will not side with the ruler of Wei.

15 The Master said, Eating simple food, drinking water, a bended arm for a pillow—there's happiness in these things too. Wealth

3 See 3:25.

4 After the death of Duke Ling of Wei in 493 B.C.E., a power struggle developed between Kuai Kui, the son of Duke Ling, who had been forced to flee from Wei, and Kuai Kui's son Che, who had been made the new ruler of Wei. Confucius's disciples, some of whom were involved with the ruling family of Wei, wished to know which party in the dispute Confucius would support. Zigong does not ask the question directly, but seeks an answer by referring to the story of Bo Yi and Shu Qi.

and eminence gained by unrightful means are to me mere drifting clouds.

16   The Master said, Give me a few more years—if I have fifty years to study, then perhaps I, too, can avoid any great errors.

[Or, according to the more widely accepted Ku text:] if I have fifty years to study the *Book of Changes*, then perhaps I, too, can avoid any great errors.

17   The Master used the correct pronunciations when speaking of the *Odes* and *Documents* or the conduct of rituals. On all such occasions, he used the correct pronunciations.[5]

18   The lord of She asked Zilu about Confucius, but Zilu did not reply.

The Master said, Why didn't you tell him that he's the kind of person who in bursts of enthusiasm forgets to eat, in his delight forgets to worry, and doesn't even realize that old age is coming on?

19   The Master said, I was not born understanding anything. A lover of antiquity, I have diligently worked to acquire understanding.

20   Subjects the Master did not discuss: strange occurrences, feats of strength, rebellion, the gods.

21   The Master said, When I walk with two others, I'm bound to find my teacher there. I single out their good points and pursue them, note their bad points and make my corrections.

22   The Master said, Heaven has implanted this virtue in me. Huan Tui—what can he do to me?[6]

23   The Master said, You young men, do you think I'm hiding something? I'm not hiding anything. I take no actions that are not taken in conjunction with you. That's Qiu for you.[7]

---

5   As opposed to the pronunciations of Confucius's native state of Lu.

6   Words said to have been spoken when Huan Tui, minister of war in the state of Song, threatened to kill him.

7   Confucius refers to himself by his personal name, Qiu.

24 The Master taught four things: culture, behavior, loyalty, trust-worthiness.

25 The Master said, A sage I have never managed to see. If I could see a true gentleman, that would be enough.

The Master said, A truly good person I have never managed to see. If I could see a person of constancy, that would be enough. With nothingness pretending to possession, emptiness pretending to fullness, want pretending to affluence, true constancy is hard to find.

26 The Master fished with a rod but not with a longline. He shot at birds with a stringed arrow, but not if they were roosting.

27 The Master said, There are those who do not have knowledge and yet make things. I'm not that way. I hear much, choose what is good and follow it, see much and keep it in mind. This is the next best thing to knowledge.

28 The people of Hu village are hard to talk to.[8] A young man came for an interview with the Master. His disciples were troubled by this.

The Master said, My concern was with what brought him, not with what he did after he left. What was so wrong about that? When a person comes to you in good faith, give him credit for the good faith. Don't expect guarantees for what comes after.

29 The Master said, Is humaneness so far away? If I want humane-ness, then humaneness is right here.

30 The minister of crime of the state of Chen asked whether Duke Zhao of Lu understood ritual. Confucius replied, Yes, he under-stood ritual.

After Confucius had retired from the scene, the minister of crime signaled to Wuma Qi to step forward and said, I have heard

---

8 Presumably a place that Confucius passed in his travels. Commentators offer various explanations as to why the villagers were hard to talk to.

that a gentleman is not partisan, but some gentlemen appear to be partisan indeed! Duke Zhao took a wife from the state of Wu, but because she was of the same surname as Duke Zhao, she was referred to simply as Wu Mengzi.[9] If Duke Zhao understood ritual, then who doesn't understand ritual?

Wuma Qi reported this to Confucius. The Master said, How fortunate I am! If I make a mistake, someone is certain to let me know.

31 If the Master was singing with others and one of them happened to be particularly good, he would invariably ask the person to repeat the piece and then he would join in.

32 The Master said, In cultural matters I believe I do as well as others. But as for personally enacting the role of the gentleman—that I am not yet up to.

33 The Master said, The title of sage or humane man—how could I dare lay claim to such? But working without tiring, teaching others and never growing weary—yes, that much could be said of me.

Gongxi Hua said, It's precisely this that we, his disciples, cannot equal him in!

34 The Master was gravely ill. Zilu asked to be allowed to offer prayers for his recovery. The Master said, Is that done? Zilu replied, Yes. The *Eulogies* say, Prayers are offered for you to the upper and lower gods and spirits.

The Master said, My praying began a long time ago.

35 The Master said, The gentleman is composed, at peace with things. The petty man is constantly fretting, fretting.

36 The Master was both mild and sharp-spoken, dignified but not oppressively so, respectful but relaxed.

9 According to Chinese ritual, persons of the same surname are forbidden to marry. The ruling houses of the states of Lu and Wu both had the Ji surname. Confucius, speaking with an official of another state, chose to give a wrong answer rather than acknowledge the error in ritual made by the ruler of his own state.

Book Eight

1   The Master said, Tai Bo may be said to exemplify the highest virtue. Three times he relinquished the right to the empire, but the common people did not understand why this was praiseworthy.

2   The Master said, Courtesy without ritual becomes labored; caution without ritual becomes timidity; daring without ritual becomes riotousness; directness without ritual becomes obtrusiveness.

   If the gentleman treats those close to him with generosity, the common people will be moved to humaneness. If he does not forget his old associates, the common people will shun cold-heartedness.

3   When Master Zeng was ill, he summoned his disciples and said, Uncover my feet, uncover my hands. The *Ode* says:

   Tremble, tremble, be wary
   as one on the brink of a deep pool,
   as one crossing thin ice—[1]

   Now and hereafter I know I have escaped, my little ones—have I not?

4   When Master Zeng was ill, Meng Jing Zi asked how he was.

   Master Zeng spoke these words: When a bird is about to die, its cries are sad. When a man is about to die, his words are good. With regard to the Way, there are three things the gentleman prizes: in his actions and manner, that he be far from harshness or arrogance; in ordering his appearance, that he stick close to trustworthiness; in his utterances, that they be far from crude or unseemly. As for the sacrificial baskets and stands, there are experts to tend to such matters.

---

1   *Book of Odes*, no. 195. Master Zeng is rejoicing that, as the ideal of filial piety dictates, he has preserved his body from harm, particularly from the mutilating punishments decreed by the penal code of ancient China.

5   Master Zeng said, Able but consulting those who lack ability, of many talents but consulting those with few, possessing but seeming to be without, full yet seeming to be empty, offended against but never retaliating—in the past I had a friend who always tried to be like that.[2]

6   Master Zeng said, Trust him as guardian to a six-foot orphan,[3] charge him with the command of a hundred-league domain, he will preside over the most critical occasions and can never be diverted from his course. This is the gentleman, is it not? This is the gentleman.

7   Master Zeng said, The man of station must be both broad-minded and resolute. His burden is heavy, and the road is long. Humaneness is the burden he is charged with—heavy, is it not? The road ends only with death—long, is it not?

8   The Master said, Get your start with the *Odes*; acquire a firm standing through ritual; complete the process with music.

9   The Master said, The common people can be made to follow a course, but cannot be made to understand why they should do so.

10   The Master said, Where there is love of daring and hatred of poverty, disorder will result. And if people lack humaneness and their hatred is extreme, disorder will result.

11   The Master said, Although one may have talents as admirable as those of the duke of Zhou, if he employs them in an arrogant or a mean manner, then whatever other qualities he has are not worth a look!

12   The Master said, Someone who can study for three years without thinking about an official salary—not easy to find!

13   The Master said, Entirely trustworthy, a lover of learning, faithful until death, exemplar of the Way, he never enters a state where

---

2   Commentators surmise that the friend was Confucius's favorite disciple, Yan Yuan.

3   A boy who has succeeded to the position of ruler of a state on the death of his father; a height of six Chinese feet would be shorter than that of a mature male.

there is peril, never remains in a state where there is disorder. When the Way prevails in the world, he appears; when the Way is lacking, he retires. When the state follows the Way, being poor and lowly is a cause for shame. When the state is without the Way, being rich and eminent is a cause for shame.

14 The Master said, If one does not hold the position, one does not dictate the policies that go with it.

15 The Master said, When Music Master Zhi has begun and reached the conclusion of the Guanju ode,[4] what a torrent of sound fills our ears!

16 The Master said, Enthusiastic but not straightforward; naive but insincere; simple, guileless, but not to be trusted—such persons I do not understand.

17 The Master said, Study as though you could never catch up, [and if you did,] you would still be fearful of losing it.

18 The Master said, Awesome was the way in which Shun and Yu held possession of the empire! Yet they took no part in it.[5]

19 The Master said, Great was Yao as a ruler! Awesome, awesome, Heaven alone is great, yet Yao alone made it his model. Vast, all-encompassing, the people could put no name to it. Awesome, awesome were his works and accomplishments, brilliant his cultural achievements.

20 Shun had five ministers, and the empire was well governed. King Wu said, I have ten capable ministers.

Confucius said, Talent is hard to find—true, is it not? In the time of Tang and Yu,[6] talent flourished, [yet Shun had only five ministers. As for King Wu's ten ministers,] one was a woman, so

4   See 3:20.
5   According to commentators, because they selected men of worth to carry out the actual administration of affairs.
6   Alternative names for the rulers Yao and Shun.

he had only nine men.[7] Zhou already possessed two-thirds of the empire, yet it continued to serve the Yin dynasty. The virtue of the Zhou may be termed the highest virtue.

21 The Master said, I can find no fault with Yu. Sparing in his food and drink, he yet served the spirits and gods with utmost filial devotion. His ordinary robes were shabby, but his sacrificial aprons and caps were of the utmost beauty. He lived in lowly rooms and halls, devoting his entire energy to the opening of irrigation ditches and channels. I can find no fault with Yu.

---

7 One woman, either King Wu's mother or his wife, was numbered among the ten ministers. The text of this passage appears faulty, and the translation is tentative.

Book Nine

1 The Master seldom spoke about profit, about fate, or about humaneness.

2 A villager of Daxiang said, What a great man Confucius is! He has studied widely, but he doesn't make any particular name for himself.

When the Master heard this, he said to his disciples, What should I specialize in? Should I specialize in charioteering? Should I specialize in archery? I think I'll specialize in charioteering.

3 The Master said, Ritual calls for caps of hemp, though nowadays silk is used, because it is more economical. I go along with others in this.

Ritual calls for one to bow at the foot of the stairs. Nowadays people bow at the top of the stairs, but this is presumptuous. Although it means differing from others, I perform the bow at the foot of the stairs.

4 The Master observed four prohibitions: no willfulness, no obstinacy, no narrow-mindedness, no egotism.

5 The Master's life was endangered in Kuang.[1] He said, King Wen is deceased, but his culture (*wen*) remains here with me. If Heaven had intended to destroy that culture, then those who come after him could not have inherited that culture. But if Heaven is not ready to destroy that culture, what can the people of Kuang do to me?

6 The prime minister[2] questioned Zigong, saying, The Master—is he a sage? He has so many capabilities!

Zigong said, Indeed, Heaven has opened the way for him to become a sage. And he has many capabilities besides.

---

1 The people of Kuang mistook Confucius for Yang Hu, a military leader who had led a revolt in the region.

2 Identity unknown; perhaps the prime minister of Wu, a state with close connections to Lu.

When the Master heard this, he said, The prime minister knows me well. When I was young, I was in humble circumstances and hence became capable in many menial undertakings. But is the true gentleman a person of many capabilities? Surely, he is not!

7 Lao reports that the Master said, I have never been given a proper trial—hence these "accomplishments."[3]

8 The Master said, Do I have knowledge? I have no special knowledge. But if an uneducated fellow comes to me with a question, I attack it with all sincerity, exploring it from end to end until I've exhausted it.

9 The Master said, The phoenix does not appear; the river puts forth no chart.[4] It is all over with me, is it not?

10 If the Master saw a person in mourning clothes, in ceremonial cap and robe, or a blind person, though the person might be younger in age, he would invariably rise to his feet and, if passing the person, would invariably quicken his steps.[5]

11 Yan Yuan, sighing, exclaimed, Look up and it's higher than ever, bore into it and it's harder still. I see it in front of me, then suddenly it's behind. Our Master—step by step, how skillfully he leads others along! He broadens me with culture, reins me in with ritual. I want to give up but cannot. Already he has exhausted my ability, yet I see him standing tall before me. But although I want to follow him, I've no way to do so.

12 The Master was gravely ill. Zilu directed the disciples to attend him in the manner of retainers.[6]

When the Master had recovered somewhat, he said, How long you go on, You, practicing these deceptions! To pretend that I

---

3 Probably a continuation of the preceding passage.

4 The appearance of the phoenix and a mysterious "chart" put forth by the Yellow River were believed to be portents signaling the presence of a sage in the world.

5 As a sign of respect.

6 As if he were a government official; as a private individual, though, he was not entitled to such retainers.

have retainers when I have no retainers—who would I be deceiving? Would I be deceiving Heaven? Moreover, rather than dying in the hands of retainers, isn't it better that I die in the hands of you, my disciples? And although I may not be entitled to a grand funeral, it's not as though I were dying by the roadside, is it?

13　Zigong said, Suppose here is a beautiful piece of jade. Better to put it in a box and store it away? Or to find someone willing to pay a good price and sell it?

　　The Master said, Sell it! Sell it! I'm waiting for a buyer.

14　The Master wished to go live among the nine foreign tribes.[7] Someone said, But they are so crude! The Master said, If a gentleman lives among them, how can they be crude?

15　The Master said, When I returned from Wei to Lu, only then was the music put in order, and the "Ya" and "Song" found their proper places.[8]

16　The Master said, In public life serving lords and high ministers; at home serving father and elder brothers; when there is a funeral, never daring to be remiss; never getting drunk and unruly—this much I can manage.

17　Standing by a stream, the Master said, It flows on like this—does it not?—never ceasing, day or night.[9]

18　The Master said, I have never seen the person who loved virtue the way he loved physical beauty.

19　The Master said, It's like building a mound. If the mound needs one more basketful of dirt for completion and I stop work, then the stopping is mine. Or it's like the case of level ground. Although it may be only one basketful of dirt, if I heap it up, then the progress is mine.

　　[Or, according to an older interpretation:]

7　Non-Chinese peoples who lived to the east of China.

8　The "Ya" and "Song" are sections of the *Book of Odes*, a text that Confucius is supposed to have edited.

9　One of the most famous passages in the *Analects*. What does it mean?

The Master said, It's like someone building a mound. If the mound needs one more basketful of dirt for completion but the person stops work, then I stop [helping him]. Or it's like the case of level ground. Although the person may have heaped up only one basketful of dirt, if he keeps working, then I follow along.

20 The Master said, Someone I could talk to and he never got tired—that was Hui, wasn't it?

21 Speaking of Yan Yuan, the Master said, What a pity! I saw him move forward. I never saw him come to a stop.

22 The Master said, There are seedlings that never grow to maturity, are there not? And mature plants that never bear fruit.[10]

23 The Master said, Respect those younger than yourself. How do you know that the coming generation may not prove as good as our present one? But if a person lives to forty or fifty and hasn't been heard of, then he's no longer worthy of respect.

24 The Master said, authoritative words—can one fail to heed them? But what is important is that they bring about a change in you. Words of friendly advice—can one fail to delight in them? But what is important is to interpret them correctly. To delight but not interpret, to heed but not change—I can do nothing with those who take that approach.

25 The Master said, Put prime value on loyalty and trustworthiness, have no friends who are not your equal, and, if you make mistakes, don't be afraid to correct them.[11]

26 The Master said, The Three Armies[12] may be stripped of their commander, but even a simple commoner cannot be deprived of his will.

27 The Master said, Wearing a shoddy floss-wadded jacket, standing beside someone clad in fox and badger furs, and feeling no shame—that would be You (Zilu)!

10 Presumed to be a meditation on the premature death of Yan Yuan.
11 Identical to the last sentence of 1:8.
12 See 7:10.

28 *Doing no harm, seeking nothing—*
  why am I not seen as good? [13]

Zilu was forever reciting these lines. The Master said, That approach—why would anyone rate it as good?

29 The Master said, When the year-end cold comes, then we know that the pine and cypress are the last to lose their leaves.

30 The Master said, The wise are never perplexed; the humane, never anxious; the brave, never afraid.

31 The Master said, You may study alongside a person but can't agree with him how to pursue the Way. You may pursue the Way with him but can't agree where to take your stand. You may agree where to take your stand but not how to adapt to circumstances.

32 *The blossoms of the cherry,*
  how they flutter and turn.
  It's not that I don't think of you,
  but your house is far away. [14]

The Master said, He doesn't really think of her. If he did, why would he worry how far it was?

13 *Book of Odes*, no. 33.

14 From a poem not found in the present text of the *Book of Odes*.

Book Ten

1   When Confucius was among the people of the community, he was mild and deferential, as though he were unable to speak. When he was in the ancestral temple of the ruler or at court, he spoke at length, though always in a circumspect manner.

2   At the morning audience, he talked with the lesser officials in a relaxed and affable way, and talked with the higher officials in a respectful manner. When the ruler made his appearance, Confucius assumed a reverential attitude, but one free of constraint.

3   When the ruler summoned him to greet a guest, his face took on a look of concentration and his pace was solemn. As he bowed and took his place with the others in line, he clasped his hands first to the left, then to the right, his robe falling front and back in graceful folds. When he hurried forward, he did so in a dignified manner. And after the guest had departed, he always reported the conclusion of the mission, saying, The guest has ceased to look back.

4   When he entered the ruler's gate, he bent forward, as though the gate were not big enough to admit him. He never stood in the middle of the gateway or stepped on the threshold.

When he passed the place customarily occupied by the ruler, his face took on a look of concentration and his pace was solemn. When he spoke, he seemed to have trouble getting out his words.

When he gathered up his robe and ascended the hall, his body was bent forward and his breathing stilled, as though he were unable to breathe. When he emerged from the audience and descended the first step, he relaxed his expression with a look of relief. When he had come to the bottom of the steps, he hurried forward in a dignified manner and returned to his original position with a reverent air.

5   When he carried the jade tablet,[1] he bent forward, as though he
could not bear the weight. He held it up as though performing a
bow, lowered it as though handing over an object. His face took
on a look of concentration, an expression of fear, and he moved
his feet carefully, as though walking a line.

When presenting official gifts, his expression was genial, and at
the exchange of private gifts his manner was even more relaxed.

6   The gentleman[2] did not wear dark purple or puce trimmings on
his garments or informal clothes of red or purple. In hot weather,
he wore a single garment of fine or coarse kudzu fiber but always
put on an outer garment when he went out. With a black robe, he
wore black lambskin; with a white robe, white deerskin; and with
a yellow robe, yellow fox fur. With informal dress, he wore fur of
ordinary length, but with the right sleeve cut somewhat shorter.
He always wore a sleeping robe one and a half times his body
length. He used thick fox or badger fur for his sitting mat. When
not in mourning, he wore any sort of belt ornament. With the
exception of ceremonial skirts, his lower garments were always
fitted at the waist. He did not wear black lambskin or a black silk
hat on visits of condolence. On the first day of the month, he invariably put on court vestments and attended court.

7   In periods of ritual purification, he always wore a clean robe made
of hemp. At such times, he invariably changed his diet and sat in a
seat different from his ordinary one.

8   He had no objection to polished rice or meat or fish finely cut up.
But if the rice was moldy or rancid, the fish putrid or the meat
spoiled, he would not eat it. If food had a bad color, he would not

---

1   Symbol of the ruler's authority.
2   This might refer to Confucius or to any proper gentleman of Confucius's time and so-
    cial station. I have translated as though it refers to Confucius, which is how it is usually
    taken.

eat it; if it smelled bad, he would not eat it; if it was improperly cooked, he would not eat it; if it was out of season, he would not eat it; if it was not properly sliced, he would not eat it; if it did not have the proper sauce, he would not eat it.

Although he might eat a large helping of meat, he did not allow it to overwhelm the vital nourishment of the rice. Only in the case of wine did he have no fixed limit, but he never drank to the point of confusion.

He would not drink wine or eat foods bought from the market. He did not refuse ginger, but did not eat much of it.

When he had received sacrificial meat from the ruler, he did not keep it until the following day. When he had meat from a family sacrifice, he ate it before the third day. If three days had passed, he would not eat it.

He did not converse at mealtime and did not talk in bed. Although it was no more than coarse grain, a soup of greens or melon, before eating he always set aside a portion as an offering and did so with a reverential air.

9   If the sitting mat was not properly straightened, he would not sit on it.

10   When drinking with the others of the community, he waited until the elderly people with canes had left before leaving. When the members of the community were performing their demon-expelling rites, he put on his court robes and stood on the eastern steps.

11   Sending a messenger to inquire about someone in another state, he would bow to the ground twice on seeing him off.

12   (Ji) Kangzi presented Confucius with some medicine. Confucius bowed to the ground in accepting it, but said, As I am not familiar with this medicine, I do not venture to taste it.[3]

---

3   Confucius politely acknowledges receipt of the gift but does not, contrary to custom, taste it, being uncertain of its properties.

13 The stables caught fire. Returning from court, the Master said, Was anyone hurt? He did not ask about the horses.

14 When the ruler sent him a gift of food, he would always straighten his sitting mat and first taste it.[4] If the ruler sent a gift of uncooked meat, he would always cook it and make an offering to the ancestors. If the ruler sent a live animal, he would raise it.

15 If he was attending the ruler at a meal, while the ruler made an offering of a portion of the food, Confucius would first taste it.

16 When he was sick and the ruler came to see him, he lay with his head to the east, his court robe spread over him, the sash draped on top.

17 When the Master entered the Grand Temple, he asked questions about everything.[5]

18 If a friend died and there was no one to receive the body, the Master would say, Let me handle the funeral proceedings. If a friend presented him with a gift, even though it might be a horse or carriage, he did not bow to the ground to receive it. Only in the case of sacrificial meat did he do so.

19 In bed, he did not sprawl like a corpse. At home, he did not behave in a formal manner.

20 If the Master saw someone in deep mourning, even though it was a person he was familiar with, he always changed his attitude. If he saw someone in a ceremonial cap or a blind person, even someone he knew well, he invariably assumed an appropriate bearing.

If he saw a person in mourning, he bowed from the crossbar of his carriage, and he would likewise bow from his carriage to a person carrying population registers.

---

4   To make certain it was safe to eat before sharing it with others.

5   Identical to the first sentence of 3:15.

Confronted with a sumptuous feast, he invariably changed his expression and rose to his feet. At a sudden clap of thunder or a blast of wind, he would invariably change his posture.

21 When mounting a carriage, he always stood in the correct position and took hold of the mounting-cord. Once in the carriage, he did not look toward the rear, speak in a hurried manner, or point at things.

22 Seeing his expression, it flew up, and after circling, came to roost.

[The Master] said,

The female pheasant on the mountain bridge—
how timely, how timely!

Zilu saluted it. It sniffed three times and flew away.[6]

---

6 This last passage is garbled somehow, and no one can make any real sense of it. Readers are advised to ignore it.

Book Eleven

1   The Master said, Older people, when it comes to rites and music, are mere rustics. Younger people, in matters of rites and music, are true gentlemen. But when it comes to usage, I follow the older people.

2   The Master said, Of those who followed me in Chen and Cai, none succeeded in gaining official position.[1]

[Or, according to another interpretation of the last phrase:] none come to my gate anymore, [because they are all dead or scattered].

[Or:] none come to my gate anymore, [because they have forgotten me].

3   VIRTUOUS CONDUCT: Yan Yuan, Min Ziqian, Ran Boniu, Zhonggong

SKILL IN LANGUAGE: Zai Wo, Zigong

ADMINISTRATIVE ABILITY: Ran You, Jilu

CULTURAL ATTAINMENT: Ziyou, Zixia

4   The Master said, Hui was not one to give me much help. Nothing I said failed to please him.

5   The Master said, What a filial son Min Ziqian is! Even with what his own father and mother and brothers say of him, people can find no fault.

6   Nan Rong kept repeating the words about the white jade tablet.[2] Confucius arranged for him to marry the daughter of his elder brother.

---

1   Because they chose to go abroad with Confucius.
2   Flaws in a white jade tablet
     can still be polished away,
     but a flaw in these words—
     nothing will mend it! (*Book of Odes*, no. 256)

7   Ji Kangzi asked, Who among your disciples loves learning? Confucius replied, There was Yan Hui—he loved learning. Regrettably, he had only a short life and is dead now. Now there is no one.

8   When Yan Yuan died, [his father] Yan Lu asked the Master if he would sell his carriage in order to provide money for an outer coffin.

   The Master said, Whether the sons are talented or untalented, each man speaks up for his own. But when [my son] Li died, I provided an inner coffin but no outer coffin. I follow the high officials—it would not be right for me to go on foot.

9   When Yan Yuan died, the Master said, Ah, Heaven is destroying me! Heaven is destroying me!

10   When Yan Yuan died, the Master mourned for him in a highly emotional manner. His followers said, Master, you are being too emotional.

   The Master said, Am I too emotional? If I am not to be emotional for this man, who should I be emotional for?

11   When Yan Yuan died, the disciples wanted to give him a lavish burial. The Master said, That won't do! But the disciples gave him a lavish burial anyway.

   The Master said, Hui looked on me as a father, but I could not bury him as I would a son. I'm not to blame—it was you young men!

12   Jilu asked how one should serve the gods and spirits. The Master said, When you don't yet know how to serve human beings, how can you serve the spirits?

   Jilu said, May I venture to ask about death? The Master said, When you don't yet understand life, how can you understand death?

13   When Min Ziqian attended the Master, his manner was highly respectful. Zilu was bold and resolute, while Ran You and Zigong

were relaxed and genial. The Master was pleased, but he said, A man like You (Zilu) will not die a natural death.[3]

14 The people of Lu were rebuilding the Long Treasury.[4] Min Ziqian said, Why not build it along the old lines? What need is there to make changes?

The Master said, This man doesn't say much, but when he does speak, he's sure to hit the mark.

15 The Master said, You's zither playing hardly fits the style of my school.[5] The other disciples began to treat Zilu with disrespect. The Master said, You is qualified to ascend the hall, though he has not yet entered the inner room.

16 Zigong asked, Of Shi (Zizhang) and Shang (Zixia), which is worthier? The Master said, Shi goes too far; Shang, not far enough.

Then Shi is the better man?

The Master said, Going too far is as bad as not going far enough.

17 The Ji family were richer than the duke of Zhou, and yet Ran Qiu, who acted as their tax collector, worked to enrich them even further.

The Master said, This man is no follower of mine! You young men, sound the drum and attack him—you have my permission!

18 ——— said, Chai (Zigao) is stupid; Shen (Zeng Shen) is dull; Shi is erratic; You is unruly.[6]

19 The Master said, Hui comes near [to the ideal], though he is often in want. Si (Zigong) holds no government office but knows how to turn a profit. His guesses often hit the mark.

---

3   Presumably, a premonition of Zilu's death in combat, which occurred in 480 B.C.E.
4   A storehouse for government supplies. Presumably, the rebuilding reflects some change in government procedures.
5   A mild criticism of the disciple Zilu, perhaps made in jest. Confucius then goes on to give a more serious evaluation of Zilu's level of attainment.
6   The speaker is not indicated, though it is usually assumed to be Confucius.

20 Zizhang asked about the way of the truly good person. The Master said, Unless you follow in others' footsteps, you cannot enter the inner room.

21 The Master said, The person skilled in argumentation—is he a true gentleman? Or merely an impressive showman?

22 Zilu asked, When I hear something, should I proceed to put it into action?

The Master said, While your father and elder brothers are alive, how can you hear something and immediately put it into action?

Ran You asked, When I hear something, should I proceed to put it into action?

The Master said, When you hear it, then act on it.

Gongxi Hua said, When You asked if, when I hear something, I should put it into action, you, Master, said, Your father and elder brothers are still alive. But when Qiu (Ran You) asked if, when I hear something, I should put it into action, you said, When you hear it, put it into action. I'm confused—may I venture to ask for an explanation?

The Master said, Qiu is timid—so I urged him on. You always tries to outdo others—so I restrained him.

23 When the Master faced danger in Kuang,[7] Yan Yuan was some distance behind. The Master said, I thought you had died!

Yan Yuan said, While the Master is alive, how would I dare to die?

24 Ji Ziran asked whether Zhongyou (Zilu) and Ran Qiu were fit to be called great ministers.[8]

The Master said, I thought that you were going to ask a quite different question, but now you ask about Zhongyou and Ran Qiu. The term "great minister" applies to someone who serves

7 See 9:5.
8 Both Zilu and Ran Qiu were in service to the Ji family. Confucius hints at the Ji family's possible designs for usurpation.

the ruler according to the Way. If he cannot do that, he retires. As for You and Qiu, they can best be called stop-gap ministers.

So you mean they would do whatever they were told to do? asked Ji Ziran.

The Master said, If it involved killing a father or a ruler, they would never go along.

25 Zilu appointed Zigao to be steward of Bi. The Master said, You are doing harm to another man's son.[9]

Zilu said, He has the people he needs and the altars of the soil and grain. Why must one read books before he is regarded as learned?

The Master said, That's why I hate smart-alecky people!

26 Zilu, Zeng Xi, Ran You, and Gongxi Hua were seated with the Master. He said, I'm a few days older than you, but forget that for the moment. You are always complaining that no one understands you. If someone truly understood you, how would you proceed?

Zilu quickly spoke up in answer: Suppose there is a state of a thousand chariots,[10] hemmed in by larger states. In addition, it's at war and thus there's a famine. If I were in charge, in three years' time I could teach the people courage and make them understand how to go about things.

The Master laughed at this and then asked Ran You how he would proceed.

He replied, An area sixty or seventy square *li*, or just fifty or sixty *li*—if I were in charge, in three years' time I could make sure that the people had enough of what they needed. As for rites and music, I'd have to wait for the help of a gentleman.

And Chi (Gongxi Zihua), how about you?

9   Bi was one of the areas under the control of the Ji family. Confucius considered Zigao too young for such an appointment, particularly one associated with the Ji family.

10 See 1:5.

I'm not saying that I could do it, he replied, but I'd like to study the procedure. In the ancestral temple, or when there is a diplomatic meeting or gathering of the rulers, I'd like to put on a ceremonial robe and cap and assist in a small way.

What about you, Dian (Zeng Xi)?

Dian ceased strumming on the large zither and, as the last notes died away, set the instrument aside and stood up. My tastes are different from those of these three men, he replied.

What harm in that? said the Master. Each person has simply to speak of his desires.

In the late spring, said Zeng Xi, when work on the spring clothes is finished, I'd like to go with five or six older fellows who have been capped and six or seven young boys to bathe in the Yi River, take the air among the altars where they pray for rain, and come home singing.

The Master gave a deep sigh and exclaimed, I'm with Dian!

When the others had left, Zeng Xi lagged behind. Master, he said, what did you think of what those three said?

The Master said, Each was just speaking of his desires, that's all.

Why did you laugh at Zilu's words?

The Master said, A state is governed through ritual, and his words lacked modesty. That's why I laughed. And as for what Ran You said, he too was talking about governing a domain, wasn't he? How can an area of sixty or seventy square *li*, or just fifty or sixty *li*, be seen as anything but a domain? And Gongxi Hua—he, too, was talking about governing a domain, wasn't he? Ceremonies in an ancestral temple or diplomatic meetings—these are carried out by feudal rulers, are they not? If Gongxi Hua is merely to "assist in a small way," I don't know who that leaves to do the big assisting.[11]

---

11   Confucius, while laughing at Zilu's outspoken manner, at the same time disparages the excessively modest language in which the other two express their ambitions.

Book Twelve

1   Yan Yuan asked about humaneness. The Master said, To master the self and return to ritual is to be humane. For one day master the self and return to ritual, and the whole world will become humane. Being humane proceeds from you yourself. How could it proceed from others?

Yan Yuan said, May I ask how to go about this?

The Master said, If it is contrary to ritual, don't look at it. If it is contrary to ritual, don't listen to it. If it is contrary to ritual, don't utter it. If it is contrary to ritual, don't do it.

Yan Yuan said, Lacking in cleverness though I am, I would like, if I may, to honor these words.

2   Zhonggong asked about humaneness. The Master said, When you go out the door, behave as though you were going to meet an important guest. When you employ the common people, do so as though you were conducting an important sacrifice. What you do not want others to do to you, do not do to others. In the domain, let there be no grievances against you; in the family, let there be no grievances against you.[1]

Zhonggong said, Lacking in cleverness though I am, I would like, if I may, to honor these words.

3   Sima Niu asked about humaneness. The Master said, The humane person is cautious about how he speaks of it.[2]

Being cautious in how you speak—is that what it means to be humane?

---

1   The domain is the feudal state of Lu. The family may refer either to the disciples' own families or to the powerful families such as the Ji, in which some of them were employed.

2   A pun on "humaneness" (ren) and "caution" (ren). Sima Niu fails to understand the meaning of Confucius's answer.

The Master said, When it is so difficult to do, how can you fail to be cautious in speaking of it?

4　Sima Niu asked about the gentleman. The Master said, A gentleman has no worries and has no fears.

Having no worries and no fears—is that what it means to be a gentleman?

The Master said, If, when he looks inside himself, he finds nothing to censure, then what could he worry about—what could he fear?

5　Sima Niu, troubled, said, All men have elder and younger brothers, but I alone have none.

Zixia said, The way I've heard it, life and death are a matter of fate; wealth and eminence rest with Heaven. If a gentleman is respectful and free of error, if he is considerate of others and treats them according to ritual, then all within the four seas are his elder and younger brothers. Why should a gentleman be troubled that he has no elder or younger brothers?

6　Zizhang asked about clear-sightedness. The Master said, Someone who is unmoved by insidious slander or hurtful and persistent accusations—he may be called clear-sighted. Someone who is unmoved by insidious slander or hurtful and persistent accusations may be called a person of far-reaching perception.

7　Zigong asked about government. The Master said, You need enough food, enough weaponry, and the trust of the common people.

Zigong said, If you had to do without one of these, which of the three would you do without first?

Do without weapons.

And if you had to do without one of the other two, which would it be?

The Master said, Do without food. From times past, everyone has to die. But without the trust of the common people, you get nowhere.

8 Ji Zicheng said, The gentleman should have solid qualities and that's enough. What need is there for refinement?[3]

Zigong said, Regrettable indeed—what you have said, sir, about the gentleman! Refinement is equal in worth to solid qualities, and solid qualities to refinement. Strip the hide of a tiger or a panther of its [patterned fur], and it is no different from that of a dog or a goat.

9 Duke Ai questioned You Ruo, saying, The crop is bad this year, and I don't have enough for government needs. What should I do?

You Ruo replied, Why not halve the rate of taxation?

The duke said, Even when I take two-tenths of the crop in taxes, I don't have enough. How could I get by with half?

You Ruo replied, If the people have enough, what ruler will be left without enough? But if the people don't have enough, how can the ruler hope to have enough?

10 Zizhang asked how to uphold virtue and detect faulty thinking.

The Master said, Concentrate on loyalty and trustworthiness and follow what is right—that's the way to uphold virtue. When you love someone, you hope that the person will live, but if you hate him, you wish that he were dead. Having wished for life, you turn around and wish for death—this is faulty thinking.[4]

11 Duke Jing of Qi questioned Confucius about government. Confucius replied, Let the ruler be a ruler; the subject, a subject; the father, a father; the son, a son.

The duke said, Splendid! For if indeed the ruler is not a ruler, the subject not a subject, the father not a father, the son not a son, then although there is grain, how will I be able to eat it?

3 See Confucius's remarks on solid qualities and refinement in 6:18. The word *wen* (refinement) has elsewhere been translated as "cultural achievements"—that is, learning, the arts.

4 The eight characters that conclude this passage, a quotation from the *Book of Odes*, make little sense here and have been left untranslated.

12 The Master said, Hearing only a word or two from the litigants, he can decide a lawsuit—that's You (Zilu), is it not?

Zilu never slept on a promise.[5]

13 The Master said, In hearing lawsuits, I'm no different from other people. What we need is for there to be no lawsuits!

14 Zizhang asked about government. The Master said, While you're engaged in it, never be negligent. Act in accordance with loyalty.

15 The Master said, Acquire broad learning in cultural matters, focus it through ritual, and you are hardly likely to go far astray—isn't that so?[6]

16 The Master said, The gentleman brings out what is most admirable in people; he does not bring out what is bad in them. The petty man does the opposite.

17 Ji Kangzi asked Confucius about government. Confucius replied, To govern is to put to rights. If you lead in the right direction, who will dare do what is not right?[7]

18 Ji Kangzi was troubled by thieves and asked Confucius for advice. Confucius replied, If you had no desires, then, even if you offered prizes, no one would steal.

19 Ji Kangzi asked Confucius about government, saying, If I kill those who don't follow the Way, and thereby encourage those who do follow the Way, how would that be?

Confucius replied, Your task is to govern. What need is there for killing? If you desire goodness, the common people will be good. The virtue of the gentleman is like the wind; the virtue of the petty people like the grass. When the wind blows over the grass, surely it will bend.

---

5   Zilu fulfilled it immediately; see 5:14.
6   Almost identical to 6:27.
7   A pun on "government" (*zheng*) and "to rectify" (*zheng*). According to commentators, Ji Kangzi was at this time serving as prime minister of Lu.

20   Zizhang asked, What does a man of station have to do to be known as accomplished?

The Master said, What do you mean by accomplished?

Zizhang replied, In the domain, invariably well reputed; in the family, invariably well reputed.

The Master said, That is reputation, not accomplishment. The accomplished man is solid, straightforward, a lover of right. He weighs people's words, observes their attitude, and is careful to defer to others. In the domain, he is invariably recognized for his accomplishments; in the family, invariably recognized for his accomplishments. The man of reputation pretends to adhere to humaneness but acts quite differently and never shows any doubt in what he's doing—so in the domain, he is invariably well reputed; in the family, invariably well reputed.

21   Fan Chi was accompanying the Master in an outing to the rain altars.[8] He said, If I may, I would like to ask how to uphold virtue, remedy badness, and detect faulty thinking.

The Master said, An excellent question! Think of the work first and the gains afterward—this is how to uphold virtue, isn't it? Attack the evils in yourself, not the evils in others—this is how to remedy badness, isn't it? Because of one morning's anger, to forget your own safety and even endanger those close to you—this is faulty thinking, isn't it?

22   Fan Chi asked about humaneness. The Master said, Love others. Fan Chi asked about understanding. The Master said, Understand others.

When Fan Chi failed to grasp the meaning, the Master said, Promote the straight, and let them oversee the crooked. That way, you can cause the crooked to be straight.

After Fan Chi had left the Master, he met Zixia. A while ago, he said, I met the Master and asked him about understanding. He said,

8   See 11:26.

Promote the straight, and let them oversee the crooked—that way you can cause the crooked to be straight. What does that mean?

Zixia said, How rich in meaning—these words! When Shun ruled the empire, he chose Gao Yao from among the multitude—and those who lacked humaneness were kept at a distance. When Tang ruled the empire, he chose Yi Yin from among the multitude—and those who lacked humaneness were kept at a distance.

23 Zigong asked how to deal with friends. The Master said, Advise them in a loyal manner; lead them with goodness. But if you get nowhere, then stop. No use to bring shame on yourself.

24 Master Zeng said, The gentleman uses the arts[9] in acquiring friends and uses friends in helping him to become humane.

9 See 1:6.

Book Thirteen

1 Zilu asked about government. The Master said, Do it by leading, and by rewarding.

Anything further, may I ask?

The Master said, Never be neglectful.

2 Zhonggong, who was serving as steward to the Ji family, asked about government.

The Master said, Your first concern should be the officers in your employ. Excuse minor shortcomings, and promote those of outstanding talent.

How can I know those of outstanding talent in order to promote them?

The Master said, Promote those you know to be worthy. As for those you don't know, will others fail to mention them?

3 Zilu said, If the ruler of Wei were waiting for you, Master, to take charge of government affairs, what would you do first?

The Master said, If I had to name my first action, I would rectify names.

Zilu said, There—that's why people say you are out of touch with reality!

The Master said, How boorish you are, You (Zilu)! When a gentleman is confronted with something he does not understand, he should adopt a respectful attitude!

If names are not rectified, then speech will not function properly, and if speech does not function properly, then undertakings will not succeed. If undertakings do not succeed, then rites and music will not flourish. If rites and music do not flourish, then punishments and penalties will not be justly administered. And if punishments and penalties are not justly administered, then the common people will not know where to place their hands and feet.

Therefore, when the gentleman names a thing, that naming can be conveyed in speech, and if it is conveyed in speech, then it can surely be put into action. When the gentleman speaks, there is nothing arbitrary in the way he does so.[1]

4 Fan Chi wanted to study how to grow grain. The Master said, In that line, I'd be less use to you than an old farmer. Fan Chi then wanted to study how to grow vegetables. The Master said, In that line, I'd be less use to you than an old vegetable grower.

After Fan Chi had left, the Master said, What a petty man, Fan Xu (Fan Chi)! If those in higher positions love ritual, then none of the common people will venture to be disrespectful. If those in higher positions love rightness, then none of the common people will venture to be disobedient. If those in higher positions love trustworthiness, then none of the common people will venture to act insincerely. And if such a condition prevails, then the people from the four lands adjacent, bearing their little children strapped to their backs, will gather around. What need to study grain growing?

5 The Master said, A man may be able to recite all three hundred odes,[2] but if you assign him as an envoy to some neighboring state and he can't give his answers unassisted, then no matter how many odes he might know, what good is he?

6 The Master said, If the person himself is correct, then although you do not order him to do so, he will act. But if the person himself is not correct, then although you order him, he will not obey.

7 The Master said, The governments of Lu and Wei are elder and younger brothers.[3]

---

1 On the rectification of names, see 12:11.

2 The three hundred–odd poems of the *Book of Odes*. They were often quoted in diplomatic gatherings, and if an official did not recognize a quotation or interpret it correctly, he could bring shame on himself and his government.

3 Lu was founded by Dan, the duke of Zhou; Wei by Kangshu, his younger brother. Both were brothers of King Wu, the founder of the Zhou dynasty. Commentators disagree about whether Confucius is referring to the friendly relations that continued to exist between the two states or to the way in which both had deteriorated in recent times.

8   The Master said of the ducal son Jing of Wei, He was good at managing his household wealth. At first he said, This just about covers things. When he had accumulated a little more, he said, Just about enough! When he became truly rich, he said, Just about perfect!

9   When the Master went to Wei, Ran You acted as his carriage driver. The Master said, A sizable population!

Ran You said, Once you have a sizable population, what should you do next?

The Master said, Make them rich!

And once they are rich?

The Master said, Instruct them!

10   The Master said, If someone were to employ me in government, in one year I could show what I can do. And in three years, I could bring things to completion.

11   The Master said, They say that if good men were to govern the domain for a hundred years, they could wipe out violence and put an end to killing. How true those words!

12   The Master said, Even if we had a true king, it would require a generation before humaneness would prevail.

13   The Master said, If you can learn to correct yourself, what trouble could you have in administering government? But if you cannot correct yourself, how can you hope to correct others?[4]

14   Master Ran came from a gathering of the court.[5] The Master said, Why are you so late?

Ran You replied, There was government business.

The Master said, Routine matters, no doubt. If there had been real government business, though I do not hold office, I would surely have been consulted.

---

4   The same play on "correct" (*zheng*) and "government" (*zheng*) as in 12:17.

5   Commentators disagree about whether the court was that of the ruler of Lu or of the Ji family.

15 Duke Ding asked, Is there one word that can bring prosperity to the domain?

Confucius replied, Words alone cannot do that. But there's a saying that might come close. People say, To be a ruler is difficult; to be a minister is not easy. If the ruler understands that it is not easy to be a ruler, this would come close, would it not, to "one word that can bring prosperity to the domain"?

And is there one word that can bring ruin to the domain? asked the duke.

Confucius replied, Words alone cannot do that. But there's a saying that might come close. People have a saying, I have no delight in being a ruler. My sole delight is making certain that no one contradicts my words.

If he is a good ruler and no one contradicts him, that would be good, would it not? But if he is not good and no one contradicts him, this would come close to being "one word that can bring ruin to the domain," would it not?

16 The lord of She asked about government. The Master said, When those close by are happy, those from far away gather around.[6]

17 When Zixia became steward of Jufu, he asked about government. The Master said, Don't try to hurry things; don't go after petty gain. Try to hurry, and you accomplish nothing. Go after petty gain, and the big undertakings won't succeed.

18 Talking with Confucius, the lord of She said, In our district there's a fellow called Honest Body. When his father stole a sheep, the son testified against him.

Confucius said, In our district the honest people are different from that. A father covers up for his son; a son covers up for his father. There's honesty in that, too.

---

6   The Chinese states of this time were eager to increase their population by attracting immigrants from other states.

19   Fan Chi asked about humaneness. The Master said, In private life, be courteous; in handling affairs, respectful; in dealings with others, loyal. Even if you go among the Yi or Di tribes,[7] these rules can never be put aside.

20   Zigong asked, How should one conduct himself in order to be called a man of station?

The Master said, Be mindful of anything shameful in your actions. When sent on a mission to other regions in the four directions, do nothing to disgrace your ruler's commands. Then you can be called a man of station.

And may I ask about a person on the next level?

The Master said, Among the members of his clan, he is praised for his filial conduct. In his village or community, he is praised for his brotherliness.

And may I ask about the next level?

The Master said, Their words are certain to be trustworthy; their actions, certain to be decisive. But petty men just plodding along can reach this level.

And how would you rate those who handle government affairs these days?

The Master said, Ah—peck and bushel people! Not even worth sizing up!

21   The Master said, If you can't get someone to work with whose actions follow the mean, then you must choose between the assertive and the cautious. The assertive will forge ahead decisively. The cautious can be trusted to have things that they will not do.

22   The Master said, Southerners have a saying: If a person lacks constancy, he cannot become a shaman or a doctor. Well put, is it not? Someone not constant in virtue is likely to suffer disgrace.[8]

---

7   See 3:5.

8   This sentence is identical to the *Book of Changes*, hexagram 32, *heng*, line 3.

And the Master said, No need to consult a diviner to know that much!

23 The Master said, The gentleman acts in harmony with others but does not ape them. The petty man apes others but is not in harmony with them.

24 Zigong asked, If everyone in the village liked him, how would that do?

The Master said, Not good enough.

If everyone in the village hated him, how would that do?

The Master said, Not good enough. Better if the good people in the village liked him, and the not-good people hated him

25 The Master said, The gentleman is easy to serve but hard to please. Try to please him with what does not accord with the Way, and he will not be pleased. But when he employs others, he thinks of their particular capabilities.

The petty man is hard to serve but easy to please. Try pleasing him with what does not accord with the Way, and he will be pleased. But when he employs others, he expects them to be able to do anything.

26 The Master said, The gentleman is self-possessed but not arrogant. The petty man is arrogant but not self-possessed.

27 The Master said, The firm, the bold, the simple, the slow in speech are near to humaneness.

28 Zilu asked, How should one conduct himself in order to be called a man of station?

The Master said, Earnest, exacting, but also harmonious—that would qualify you to be called a man of station. With friends, earnest, exacting. With elder and younger brothers, harmonious.

29 The Master said, Let a good man instruct them for seven years, and the common people will be capable of military service.

30 The Master said, To fail to instruct the common people in warfare—you could call that throwing them away.

Book Fourteen

1   Xian (Yuan Si) asked what is shameful. The Master said, When a state follows the Way, one receives an official stipend. But when a state is without the Way, to receive an official stipend is shameful.

2   [Yuan Si said,] If one is free of high-handedness, bragging, enmity, and craving, can this be termed humaneness? The Master said, It may be termed difficult. But as for humaneness—I don't know about that.

3   The Master said, A man of station who longs for the comforts of home does not deserve to be called a man of station.

4   The Master said, When a state follows the Way, be stern in speech, stern in action. When a state is without the Way, be stern in action but conciliatory in speech.

5   The Master said, Those who have virtue invariably have something to say, but those who have something to say do not invariably have virtue. Those who are humane are invariably courageous, but those who are courageous are not invariably humane.

6   Nangong Kuo questioned Confucius, saying, Yi was a skilled archer and Ao could push a boat over dry land, but neither was able to die a natural death. Yu and Ji, however, though they worked the fields in person, gained possession of the empire. The Master made no reply.

    After Nangong Kuo had left, the Master said, A gentleman should be like this! An upholder of virtue should be like this![1]

7   The Master said, A gentleman but not humane—there are some like that, are there not? But there's never been a petty man who was humane.

8   The Master said, If you love people, can you fail to reward them? If you are loyal to them, can you fail to admonish them?

1   Confucius admires Nangong Kuo for recognizing the worth of the sage ruler Yu and the minister Ji.

9   The Master said, When government proclamations were being drawn up, Pi Chen made the first draft; Shi Shu examined it; Ziyu, the official in charge of envoys, polished it; and Zichan of Dongli added the finishing touches.[2]

10 Someone asked about Zichan. The Master said, A generous man.

The person asked about Zixi. The Master said, That man! That man!

The person asked about Guan Zhong.[3] The Master said, He was the one who stripped the leader of the Bo family of Pian, a village of three hundred households, so that he had to eat meager fare, though until his death he never spoke a resentful word.

11 The Master said, To be poor but not resentful is difficult. To be rich and not arrogant is easy.

12 The Master said, Meng Gongchuo would have been excellent as chief retainer to the powerful Zhao or Wei family. But he could not have served as a high official even in the little states of Deng and Xue.

13 Zilu asked about the complete person. The Master said, Zang Wu-zhong's understanding, Meng Gongchuo's freedom from desire, the valor of Zhuangzi of Pian, the arts of Ran Qiu—embellish them through rites and music, and you have what may be termed the complete person.

And he said, But the complete person of our times need not necessarily be like this. If when he spies gain, he remembers what is right; when he spies danger, is ready to risk his life; when faced with old promises, does not forget his past words; then he can be termed a complete person.

---

2   Confucius wishes to depict good government as operating through written documents drawn up by high-ranking members of the bureaucracy, such as these eminent officials of the state of Zheng in the preceding generation.

3   Not enough is known about the officials Zixi and Guan Zhong to determine the exact meaning of Confucius's comments.

14 The Master questioned Gongming Jia about Gongshu Wenzi, saying, Is it true that your master never spoke, never laughed, and never accepted things?

Gongming Jia replied, Whoever told you that was exaggerating. My master spoke only when it was time to do so—thus others did not object to his speaking. He laughed only when he was happy—so others did not object to his laughter. He accepted things only when it was right to do so—thus others did not object to his accepting.

The Master said, Is that so? Could that really be so?

15 The Master said, Zang Wuzhong holed up in Fang and asked the ruler of Lu to appoint [his brother] Wei as heir to succeed him. Although they say he did not press the ruler to do so, I do not believe that.[4]

16 The Master said, Duke Wen of Jin used devious methods, not upright ones. Duke Huan of Qi used upright methods, not devious ones.[5]

17 Zilu said, When Duke Huan put to death his brother, the ducal son Jiu, Shao Hu died with him but Guan Zhong did not.[6] That was hardly humane of Guan Zhong, was it?

The Master said, Duke Huan nine times called the other feudal rulers together in assembly and did so without employing his war chariots. Guan Zhong's influence made this possible. But as for his humaneness, as for his humaneness—

---

4   Zang Wuzhong, involved in a power struggle within Lu, was forced to flee to a neighboring state in 546 B.C.E. Before he did so, he paused in his domain of Fang and asked the Lu ruler to appoint his brother to succeed him as leader of the Zang family. Although people said he did not pressure the ruler of Lu to do so, Confucius believed otherwise.

5   Both Duke Wen and Duke Huan were *ba* (hegemons) who for a time exercised power over the other feudal rulers. Just what Confucius is referring to in his comment is unclear.

6   Both Shao Hu and Guan Zhong had been supporters of Jiu, but after Jiu's death Guan Zhong transferred his loyalty to Duke Huan.

18 Zigong said, Guan Zhong was not a humane man, was he? When Duke Huan put to death the ducal son Jiu, he not only could not bring himself to die with Jiu but went on to become prime minister to Duke Huan.

The Master said, With Guan Zhong as his prime minister, Duke Huan was able to become leader of the feudal lords and impose order on the empire. Even to this day, our people benefit from what he did. Without Guan Zhong, we would be wearing our hair unbound and folding our robes to the left.[7] Would you expect of him the kind of "fidelity" of ordinary men or women who strangle themselves, end up in a roadside ditch, with no one even aware of it?

19 Zhuan had been a retainer to Gongshu Wenzi, but later he became a high official, taking a place beside Wenzi in the service of the ruler. When the Master heard of this, he said, Gongshu Wenzi deserves the posthumous name Cultured (Wen).[8]

20 Speaking of Duke Ling of Wei, the Master said that he lacked the Way.

Ji Kangzi said, If so, why doesn't he meet with failure?

Confucius said, He has Zhongshu Yu (Gongshu Wenzi) to receive foreign envoys, Invocator Tuo to supervise the ancestral temples, and Wangsun Jia to handle military affairs. Given such conditions, how could he fail?

21 The Master said, He who speaks irresponsibly will find it hard to put his words into action.

22 Chen Chengzi assassinated Duke Jian of Qi. Confucius bathed, washed his hair, proceeded to court, and reported to Duke Ai,

---

7 Non-Chinese customs; that is, China would have been invaded by foreign tribes and Chinese culture wiped out.

8 On Gongshu Wenzi's posthumous name, see 5:15. Confucius applauds Gongshu Wenzi for having allowed his former retainer to become equal to himself as an official in the service of the ruler of Wei.

saying, Chen Heng (Chen Chengzi) has assassinated his ruler. I request that he be punished.

The duke said, Report that to the three leaders of the Ji family.

Later Confucius said, I follow the high officials—I would not dare to leave such an event unreported. The ruler said, Report that to the three leaders of the Ji family.

When he went and reported to the three leaders, they declined to act. Confucius said, I follow the high officials—I would not dare to leave such an event unreported.[9]

23 Zilu asked how to serve the ruler. The Master said, Never deceive him; oppose him openly.

24 The Master said, The gentleman is an expert in important matters; the petty man, an expert in trivial ones.

25 The Master said, Formerly people studied to improve themselves; now they do so to impress others.

26 Qu Boyu sent a messenger to Confucius. Confucius seated him at his side and questioned him, saying, What does your master do?

The messenger replied, My master endeavors to lessen his faults, though he is not yet entirely successful.

After the messenger left, the Master said, What a messenger, what a messenger![10]

27 The Master said, If one does not hold the position, one does not dictate the policies that go with it.[11]

28 Master Zeng said, The gentleman's thoughts do not extend beyond the position that he holds.

---

9 Duke Jian of Qi was assassinated in 481 B.C.E., when Confucius was seventy-two by Chinese reckoning. Duke Ai, a weak ruler, showed no inclination to launch a military strike against Chen Heng, leader of the powerful Chen (Tian) ministerial family of Qi, nor did the heads of the Ji family. In the years following Confucius's death, the process of usurpation in Qi continued until 386 B.C.E., when the Tian family overthrew the ruling family and declared itself ruler of Qi.

10 Some commentators take Confucius's final remark as an indication of approval, while others see it as sarcasm.

11 Identical to 8:14.

29 The Master said, The gentleman is ashamed to let his words outstrip his actions.

30 The Master said, The Way of the gentleman has three characteristics that are still beyond me. The humane are never anxious; the wise, never perplexed; the brave, never afraid.[12]

Zigong said, Master, that is your own Way.

31 Zigong was voicing his opinion of others. The Master said, How wise Si (Zigong) is! I'm afraid I don't have time for that sort of thing.

32 The Master said, Don't worry about others' not understanding you. Worry about your own lack of ability.

33 The Master said, Do not be overly wary of deception; do not suspect others of bad faith. But he who is first to perceive the true situation is the wise one!

34 Weisheng Mu said to Confucius, Qiu, why are you always rushing around? Are you trying to talk yourself into favor?[13]

Confucius replied, I would not venture to talk myself into favor. I'm distressed by so much obstinacy.

35 The Master said, The famous horse Qi was praised not for his strength but for his virtue.[14]

36 Someone said, Repay hatred with virtue—how would that do?

The Master said, Then how would you repay virtue? Repay hatred with uprightness. Repay virtue with virtue.

37 The Master said, No one understands me—isn't that so?

Zigong said, Why do you suppose that no one understands you?

12 Almost identical to 9:30.

13 The fact that Weisheng Mu addresses Confucius by his personal name, Qiu, suggests that he is older than Confucius or disdainful of him. He is referring to the way Confucius travels from state to state in an effort to gain a hearing for his ideas.

14 Virtue in the sense of innate nature or capacity.

The Master said, I bear no grudge against Heaven; I do not blame others. I study affairs close at hand and try to become adept in higher matters. Perhaps it is Heaven that understands me!

38 Gongbo Liao spoke ill of Zilu to the head of the Ji family. Zifu Jingbo reported this, saying, My master[, Ji Sun,] has for some time been led astray by Gongbo Liao. But I still have enough influence to see that Gongbo Liao is executed and his corpse exposed in the marketplace.

The Master said, If the Way is destined to proceed, that is a matter of fate. And if the Way is destined to fail, that too is fate. How can Gongbo Liao change what is fated?

39 The Master said, Worthy persons retire from the world. The next best retire from the region. The next best retire because of a look. The next best retire because of a word.

The Master said, There were seven who did so.[15]

40 Zilu stopped for the night at Stone Gate. The gatekeeper said, Where are you from? Zilu said, From the household of Confucius.

The gatekeeper said, The one who knows there's nothing that can be done but keeps on trying?

41 When he was in Wei, the Master was once playing the chiming stones.[16] A man carrying a basket passed the gate of the house where Confucius was staying. He said, Someone of strong convictions is sounding the stones! After a while he said, Shallow—all this clang-clanging! If no one understands you, you give up, that's all.

In deep water, let your robe get wet;
In shallow, hike it up.[17]

The Master said, Quite right—that would be the easy way out.

---

15   The passage refers to recluses and how much animosity one should put up with before retiring and becoming one. Who the "seven" are is not known; the text is probably faulty.

16   A row of stone slabs suspended from a rack and sounded with a mallet.

17   *Book of Odes*, no. 34, which refers to adjusting to circumstances.

42 Zizhang said, The *Book of Documents* states that Gao Zong was in his mourning hut for three years without speaking.[18] What does this mean?

The Master said, Why only Gao Zong? The men of ancient times all did this. When the ruler passed away, the officials under him for three years took all their instructions from the prime minister.

43 The Master said, If those in high positions love ritual, the common people will be easy to employ.

44 Zilu asked about the gentleman. The Master said, He trains himself to be respectful.

Is that all?

The Master said, He trains himself in order to give ease to others.

Is that all?

The Master said, He trains himself in order to give ease to all men and women. But training himself in order to give ease to all men and women—even the sages Yao and Shun found that hard to do.

45 Yuan Rang sat waiting for Confucius in a slovenly posture. The Master said, Young but not properly submissive, grown and no one speaks well of you, old and you still don't die—a real pest!

He rapped on Yuan's shins with his cane.[19]

46 A young boy of the village of Que was assigned to carry messages. Someone asked Confucius about him, saying, Is he improving himself?

The Master said, I've seen him sit in the seat for adults, seen him walk shoulder to shoulder with his elders. He's not trying to improve himself—he's just in a hurry to be treated as a grownup.

18 The passage alludes to the three-year mourning period for parents, here observed by Gao Zong for his father, the former ruler of the Yin dynasty. Zizhang is probably referring to the *Book of Documents*, Zhou Documents, "Wuyi."

19 Was Confucius serious in his censures of his old friend Yuan Rang, one wonders, or merely joking?

Book Fifteen

1 Duke Ling of Wei asked Confucius about battle formations. Confucius replied, With regard to sacrificial platters and stands, I have some learning. But I have never studied military affairs.

The next day he left Wei for good.

2 When Confucius was in Chen, he ran out of provisions and his followers were so weak that none of them could stand up. Zilu confronted Confucius angrily, saying, Does the gentleman have to put up with such hardships?

The Master said, The gentleman remains firm in the face of hardships. The petty man, when he encounters hardship, gives way to panic.

3 The Master said, Si (Zigong), you suppose that I have studied many different matters and retain them in my memory, don't you?

Zigong replied, Yes. Isn't that so?

The Master said, No. I have one thread that links it all together.[1]

4 The Master said, You (Zilu), those who understand virtue are few!

5 The Master said, Of those who ruled through inaction, surely Shun was one. What did he do? Dedicating himself to courtesy, he faced directly south, that was all.[2]

6 Zizhang asked about how to get along in the world. The Master said, If your words are loyal and trustworthy and your actions

---

1 See 4:15.

2 Confucius is invoking the Daoist ideal of *wuwei* (inaction) in characterizing the rule of the ancient sage Shun. But Shun, being a sage, was already possessed of very powerful charisma and, according to legend, was assisted by highly capable ministers. The Chinese ruler traditionally sits facing south.

sincere and respectful, then even in the lands of the Man and Mo tribes you will get along.[3] But if your words are not loyal and trustworthy and your actions not sincere and respectful, then even in your own district or village you won't get along, will you? When you stand up, see these words plainly before you; when riding in your carriage, see them resting on the crossbar. Act in this way and then you will get along.

Zizhang wrote this down on his sash.

7 The Master said, How upright Shi Yu was! When the state followed the Way, he was straight as an arrow. When the state was without the Way, he was straight as an arrow. What a gentleman Qu Boyu was! When the state followed the Way, he held office. When the state was without the Way, he knew how to fold up his hopes and put them away in the breast of his robe.

8 The Master said, If it's someone you ought to speak to and you fail to speak, you waste a person. If it's someone you ought not to speak to and you speak, you waste words. The wise man doesn't waste people and doesn't waste words either.

9 The Master said, The man of high ideals, the humane person, never tries to go on living if it is harmful to humaneness. There are times when he sacrifices his life to preserve humaneness.

10 Zigong asked how to practice humaneness. The Master said, A craftsman who wants to do his job well must first sharpen his tools. Whatever country you are in, be of service to the high officials who are worthy and become friends with the men of station who are humane.

11 Yan Yuan asked about how to order the state. The Master said, Use the Xia calendar, ride in the chariots of the Yin, wear the caps of the Zhou, and for music, the Shao and Wu. Do away with the

---

3 The Man and Mo were non-Chinese peoples who lived to the south and north of the Chinese.

Zheng tunes and stay away from artful talkers. The Zheng tunes are excessive, and artful talkers are dangerous.[4]

12 The Master said, The person who fails to take far-reaching precautions is sure to encounter near-at-hand woes.

13 The Master said, It's hopeless! I have never seen the person who loved virtue the way he loved physical beauty.[5]

14 The Master said, Zang Wenzhong held high office unjustly, did he not? He knew that Liuxia Hui was a man of worth, but failed to elevate him to a position comparable to his own.[6]

15 The Master said, Be hard on yourself; go lightly when you blame others—that way you stay clear of resentment.

16 The Master said, People who don't ask themselves, How should I proceed? How should I proceed?—I don't know how to proceed with their kind!

17 The Master said, Groups gathered together all day, not a word touching what is right, happy in carrying out their petty schemes—don't look for much from them!

18 The Master said, The gentleman makes rightness the substance, practices it through ritual, displays it with humility, brings it to completion with trustworthiness. That's the gentleman.

19 The Master said, The gentleman is troubled by his own lack of ability. He is not troubled by the fact that others do not understand him.

20 The Master said, The gentleman is pained to think that after he has left the world his name will not be remembered.

21 The Master said, The gentleman makes demands on himself. The petty man makes demands on others.

4   On the Shao and Wu music, see 3:25. The words to the songs of the state of Zheng are found in the *Book of Odes*, but Confucius apparently disapproved of the music to which they were sung.

5   Identical to 9:18.

6   On Zang Wenzhong, at one time prime minister of the state of Lu, see 5:18.

22 The Master said, The gentleman is proud but not contentious; he joins with others but is not cliquish.

23 The Master said, The gentleman does not esteem a person merely because of his words, nor does he disregard words merely because of the person.

24 Zigong asked, Is there a single word that can guide a person's conduct throughout life?

    The Master said, That would be reciprocity, wouldn't it? What you do not want others to do to you, do not do to others.[7]

25 The Master said, In my dealings with others, who have I censured, who have I praised? If I praise someone, it is because he has been put to the test. The common people of today are the ones who carried out the straight Way of the Three Dynasties.[8]

26 The Master said, I can still remember when recorders left blanks in their text [when they were unsure of something,] or when people with horses lent them to others to drive. Nowadays such customs are no longer observed, are they?[9]

27 The Master said, Clever words are the disrupters of virtue. Lack patience in minor matters, and you may disrupt larger schemes.

28 The Master said, When everyone hates someone, look into the matter carefully. When everyone likes someone, look into the matter carefully.[10]

29 The Master said, A person can enlarge the Way, but the Way cannot enlarge a person.

30 The Master said, To make a mistake and not correct it is to make a mistake indeed.

---

7   See 12:2.
8   The Xia, Yin, and Zhou, particularly the early, well-ordered years of these dynasties. That is, the common people of Confucius's time are the same as those of the golden ages of the past.
9   The meaning of the passage is unclear.
10 See 13:24.

31 The Master said, Once I went all day without eating and all night without sleeping in order to think. It was no use—better to study.

32 The Master said, The gentleman schemes for the Way; he does not scheme for food. You might work the fields and still at times encounter hunger; you might study and at times acquire an official stipend. But the gentleman worries about the Way; he does not worry about poverty.

33 The Master said, You might have sufficient knowledge to gain a position, but if you do not have the humaneness needed to hold on to it, then although you gain it, you will surely lose it. You might have sufficient knowledge to gain a position and the humaneness needed to hold on to it, but if you do not administer it with dignity, the common people will not respect you. You might have sufficient knowledge to gain a position, the humaneness needed to hold on to it, and may administer it with dignity, but if your actions do not accord with ritual, the results will be less than good.

34 The Master said, The gentleman cannot handle affairs demanding only limited understanding, but he is capable of large undertakings. The petty man is not capable of large undertakings, but he can handle affairs demanding limited understanding.

35 The Master said, Humaneness is more vital to the people than water or fire. I have seen people die from treading on water or fire, but I have never seen the person who died from treading the path of humaneness.

36 The Master said, In matters of humaneness, do not defer even to your teacher.

37 The Master said, The gentleman is firm but not stubbornly unbending.

38 The Master said, In serving the ruler, attend respectfully to your duties and look on pay as a secondary matter.

39 The Master said, In matters of instruction, there should be no class distinctions.

40 The Master said, If your Way is not the same, you cannot lay plans for one another.

41 The Master said, With words it is enough if they get the meaning across.

42 Music Master Mian called on Confucius. When they reached the steps, the Master said, Here are the steps. When they reached the seating mats, the Master said, Here are the mats. After everyone was seated, the Master reported, So-and-so is over here. So-and-so is over there.

After Music Master Mian had left, Zizhang asked, Is that the way one talks to a music master? The Master said, Yes, of course. That's how one assists a music master.[11]

---

[11] The music masters of Confucius's time were blind.

Book Sixteen

[In the following passage Ran You and Zilu, two disciples who were in the service of the Ji family, inform Confucius of a plan to attack Zhuanyu, a small feudal domain within the state of Lu. It was situated close to Bi, a region under the control of the Ji family. Feudal lords were charged with the duty of sacrificing to the major mountains and rivers in their domain.]

When the Ji family was about to attack Zhuanyu, Ran You and Jilu (Zilu) called on Confucius and reported that the Ji family was planning to move against Zhuanyu.

Confucius said, Qiu (Ran You), are you going to make a mistake like this? Long ago the kings of former times charged Zhuanyu with the duty of conducting sacrifices to Mount Dongmeng. Moreover, it is located within our state and thus is a servant of our altars of the soil and grain. What reason could there be to attack it?

Ran You said, Our lord wishes to do so. Neither of us, his servants, wish it.

Confucius said, Zhou Ren had a saying: Show your ability, move into the ranks; if you can't do that, then step aside. If you see your lord in danger and cannot support him, if you see him tottering and cannot prop him up, then of what use are you as his aides? And you are wrong in what you said. If the tiger or rhinoceros breaks out of its cage, if the tortoiseshell or jades lie broken in their box, whose fault is it?[1]

Ran You said, Zhuanyu is at present heavily fortified and is located close to Bi. If we do not seize it now, it is bound to be a threat to our lord's sons and grandsons.

---

[1]   The fault of the person responsible, as you are responsible for the actions of the Ji family.

Confucius said, The gentleman hates someone who won't say outright that he favors a course and yet keeps offering reasons to support it. I have heard that a nation or a family does not worry that it has little but that that little is unevenly apportioned, does not worry that it is poor but that it is unstable. Because with equitable distribution there is no real poverty, with harmony, no real scarcity, with stability, no real peril. When such a situation exists, if neighboring people do not submit to your ruler, then enhance your culture and virtue and draw them to you, and once you have drawn them to you, offer them stability. Now you, Qiu and You, in assisting your lord to deal with neighbors who do not submit, are not following a course that will draw them to you. Instead, the state threatens to break apart, to collapse, and you cannot hold it together. And now you propose to resort to armed conflict within the state itself. I fear that the threat to the Ji family lies not in Zhuanyu but in what is taking place within its own walls!

2   Confucius said, When the Way prevails in the world, rites, music, and punitive expeditions proceed from the Son of Heaven. When the Way no longer prevails in the world, rites, music, and punitive expeditions proceed from the feudal lords, and rarely does this situation continue for ten generations before failure ensues. If these proceed from the high officials, rarely five generations pass before failure; and if the retainers of the high officials govern the fate of the nation, rarely three generations before failure. When the Way prevails in the world, government is not in the hands of the high officials. When the Way prevails in the world, ordinary people voice no criticisms.

3   Confucius said, Five generations have gone by since the right of making awards passed out of the hands of the ducal house of Lu, and four generations since the power of government came to be

exercised by the high officials.[2] Therefore, the three houses that descend from Duke Huan of Lu are now growing powerless.

4 Confucius said, Three kinds of friends are beneficial; three kinds are harmful. Straightforward friends, sincere friends, well-informed friends—these are beneficial. Hypocritical friends, sycophantic friends, glib-talking friends—these are harmful.

5 Confucius said, Three kinds of delight are beneficial; three kinds are harmful. The delight of regulating oneself with rites and music, the delight of speaking of others' good points, the delight of having many worthy friends—these are beneficial. Delight in extravagant pleasures, delight in idle wanderings, delight in the joys of the feast—these are harmful.

6 Confucius said, In one's relations with a gentleman, there are three errors to avoid. To speak of something before the time is right—this is called boorishness. To fail to speak when it is time to do so—this is called secretiveness. To speak without first observing the face of the person one is addressing—this is called blindness.

7 Confucius said, The gentleman has three things to beware of. When he is young and his energies are not fully controlled, he bewares of sexual attraction. When he is mature and his energies are at their height, he bewares of aggressiveness. When he is old and his energies have waned, he bewares of avariciousness.

8 Confucius said, The gentleman has three things he stands in awe of. He stands in awe of the Mandate of Heaven, of persons in high position, and of the words of the sages. The petty man, failing to understand the Mandate of Heaven, does not view it with awe. He treats persons in high position with disrespect and scorns the words of the sages.

---

2   That is, the three branches of the Ji family, the three houses descended from Duke Huan referred to in the next sentence.

9   Confucius said, Those born with understanding rank highest. Those who study and gain understanding come next. Those who face difficulties and yet study—they are next. Those who face difficulties but never study—they are the lowest type of people.

10 Confucius said, The gentleman has nine things he thinks of. He thinks—is my vision clear? He thinks—is my hearing acute? He thinks—is my expression genial? He thinks—is my manner courteous? He thinks—are my words loyal? He thinks—am I respectful in the way I serve? He thinks—when in doubt, do I seek advice? He thinks—when angry, do I think of the troubles that may ensue? He thinks—when I spy gain, would I be right to take it?

11 Confucius said, He sees what is good and acts as though he could never attain it, sees what is not good and acts as though he had put his hand in scalding water—I've seen people like that and heard reports of their kind. He lives in seclusion in order to fulfill his aims, practices rightness in order to perfect his Way—I've heard reports of such people but never actually seen them.

12 Duke Jing of Qi had a thousand teams of four horses, but the day he died, the common people of Qi could think of no bounty to praise him for. Bo Yi and Shu Qi died of hunger on Mount Shouyang, yet to this day the common people praise them. This is what the saying means.[3]

13 Chen Gang (Ziqin) questioned [Confucius's son] Boyu, saying, As a son, have you received any special instruction?

No, replied Boyu. But once, when my father was standing by himself and I hurried across the courtyard, he said, Have you studied the *Odes*? Not yet, I replied. He said, If you don't study the *Odes*, you won't know how to speak properly! So after that I studied the *Odes*. Another day, when he was standing by himself

3   This passage appears to be defective, as it lacks any indication of the speaker or the "saying" to which the last sentence refers.

and I hurried across the courtyard, he said, Have you studied the rites? Not yet, I replied. He said, If you don't study the rites, you won't have any basis to stand on. So after that I studied the rites. He gave me these two pieces of instruction.

Afterward Chen Gang, delighted, said, I asked one question and learned three things. I learned about the *Odes*, I learned about rites, and I learned that the gentleman maintains a certain distance in relations with his son.

14 In the case of the wife of the ruler of a state, the ruler refers to her as "the lady," and she refers to herself as "this little youth." The people of the state refer to her as "the lord's lady," but when they are addressing persons of other states, they call her "our little lord." The people of other states refer to her as "the lord's lady."[4]

---

4   This seems to be a passage from a text on ritual that has for some reason been appended here.

Book Seventeen

1 Yang Huo (Yang Hu?) wanted to see Confucius, but Confucius refused to see him. He then sent Confucius a suckling pig. Confucius, choosing a time when Yang was not at home, went to express thanks for the gift, but he happened to meet Yang in the street. Addressing Confucius, Yang Huo said, Come—I have something to say to you. You hide in your heart a wealth of talent and yet let your country go astray. Can that be called humaneness? Of course not! You long to hold office and yet time and again miss the chance to do so. Can that be called wisdom? Of course not! The days and months fly by, time does not work in our favor!

Confucius said, Very well—I will take public office.

2 The Master said, In nature close to one another, in practice far apart.[1]

3 The Master said, Only the highest among the wise and the lowest among the stupid never change.

4 When the Master visited Wucheng, he listened to the music of stringed instruments and a chorus. A smile came to his face, and he said, To cut up a chicken, why use an ox-cleaver?

Ziyou replied, In the past I have heard you say, Master, that when the gentleman studies the Way, he learns to love others, and when the petty man studies the Way, he becomes easy to employ.

The Master said, You young men, what Yan (Ziyou) says is right. My earlier remark was just meant as a joke.[2]

---

1   Confucius's statement on the human condition.
2   Ziyou, as we have seen in 6:14, had been made steward of the outlying region of Wucheng. Confucius's remark on the knife used to cut up a chicken is usually interpreted to mean that the music performed for him in Wucheng was overly pretentious. Another interpretation would take it to mean that a man of Ziyou's talents is wasted on a minor post in Wucheng.

5   Gongshan Furao headed a rebellion in the region of Bi and in-
    vited Confucius to join him.³ The Master wanted to go, but Zilu,
    displeased, said, Don't go, and that will end the matter. What
    need is there to join someone like Gongshan?

    The Master said, He has invited me—how could it be a com-
    plete waste? If someone would only make use of me, I could cre-
    ate a Zhou of the east!⁴

6   Zizhang asked Confucius about humaneness. Confucius said, A
    person who can exercise these five in his dealings with the world
    is acting humanely.

    When Zizhang asked what "these five" were, Confucius said,
    Courtesy, tolerance, trustworthiness, diligence, and kindness. Be
    courteous, and you avoid disrespect. Be tolerant, and you win
    over the multitude. Be trustworthy, and you are trusted by others.
    Be diligent, and your work will go well. Be kind, and you will be
    able to employ others.

7   Bi Xi invited the Master to join him, and the Master wanted to
    go.⁵ Zilu said, In the past I have heard you say, When someone is
    personally doing what is not good, the gentleman will not go near
    him. Bi Xi has raised a revolt in Zhongmou. What reason could
    you have to go there?

    The Master said, You are right—that's what I said. But don't
    people say, So hard, file it, but it never wears thin? And don't they
    say, So white, dirty it, but it never turns black? Am I some sort of
    bitter melon? Can I go on hanging here and never be eaten?

3   Gongshan Furao, like Yang Hu, had been a retainer of the Ji family, but in 502 B.C.E. he
    declared himself in revolt against them. Confucius perhaps thought that he was intend-
    ing to restore power to the ruler of Lu.

4   That is, Confucius could establish in the eastern state of Lu an ideal regime such as
    characterized the early Zhou dynasty.

5   Bi Xi, like Gongshan Furao, had started a revolt, this one in Zhongmou in an area con-
    trolled by the state of Jin, and had summoned Confucius to join him. Once again, Con-
    fucius saw this as a possible chance to put his ideals into practice.

8 The Master said, You (Zilu), have you heard of the six terms and the six flaws attending them?

Zilu replied, No, not yet.

Sit down, said the Master, and I will tell you. Love of humaneness without love of study invites the flaw of foolishness. Love of understanding without love of study invites the flaw of recklessness. Love of trustworthiness without love of study invites the flaw of injurious behavior. Love of uprightness without love of study invites the flaw of bluntness. Love of bravery without love of study invites the flaw of riotousness. Love of firmness without love of study invites the flaw of irrational action.

9 The Master said, Young people, why do none of you study the *Odes*? The *Odes* train you in analogy, allow you to observe customs, teach you to be sociable, teach you to express anger. Close at hand, you learn how to serve your father; in more distant terms, how to serve the ruler. And you become familiar with the names of numerous birds, animals, plants, and trees.

10 The Master said to [his son] Boyu, Have you studied the "Zhounan" and "Shaonan"?[6] Anyone who doesn't know the "Zhounan" and "Shaonan" is like a person who stands with a wall in front of him.

11 The Master said, Ritual! ritual! they say. But is it just a matter of jades and silks? Music! music! they say. But is it just a matter of bells and drums?

12 The Master said, Stern in aspect but weak inside—look for his likeness among petty men, and it would be the thief who breaks through or climbs over walls.

13 The Master said, The self-righteous villager is the thief of virtue.

14 The Master said, Hear it along the road and expound it in the byways—this is to throw virtue away.[7]

6   The first and second sections of the *Book of Odes*.

7   That is, come on some good idea and, before you understand it fully, begin expounding it to others.

15 The Master said, Can you serve the ruler with some mean-minded fellow as your companion? Before he has gotten what he wants, he worries he won't get it. After he has gotten it, he worries he'll lose it. And when he starts worrying about losing it, there's nothing he won't do!

16 The Master said, In former times the common people had three weaknesses, but now even these seem to have largely disappeared.[8] Assertive persons in the past were reckless; now they are downright overbearing. Firm-minded persons in the past were prudish; now they are testy and belligerent. Stupid persons in the past were at least upright; now all they do is try to deceive others.

17 The Master said, Clever words and a pleasing countenance—little humaneness there.[9]

18 The Master said, I hate the way the color purple detracts from red. I hate the way the tunes of Zheng throw the Ya music into confusion.[10] I hate the way clever talkers bring ruin to the state and the leading families.

19 The Master said, I wish I could just say nothing. Zigong said, But Master, if you do not say anything, what will we, your followers, have to pass on to others?

The Master said, What does Heaven say? The four seasons proceed in order, the hundred creatures live their lives, but what does Heaven say?

20 Ru Bei wanted to visit Confucius, but Confucius excused himself on the grounds of illness. Then, as the person who had delivered the message was going out the door, Confucius took up his zither and began to sing, making certain that the man heard him.

---

8 The weaknesses turn out to have been better than the traits that have supplanted them.

9 Identical to 1:3.

10 On the music of the state of Zheng, see 15:11. The Ya music is the elegant court music used to accompany the songs in the "Ya" section of the *Book of Odes*.

21   Zai Wo asked about the three-year mourning period, saying that one year should be long enough.[11] If the gentleman goes three years without performing rituals, the rituals are certain to decline; if he goes three years without performing music, music is certain to be lost. The old grain has been used up; the new grain has ripened; drills have kindled new fires to replace the old ones—surely one year is long enough!

  The Master said, Eating rice, wearing brocade—would you feel right doing that?

  Yes, I would, said Zai Wo.

  If you would feel right, then do so. But when a gentleman is in mourning, if he ate fine food, it would have no savor; if he listened to music, it would bring no joy; if he lived in ease, it would not feel right. Therefore, he does not do so. But now you would feel right, so you may do so.

  After Zai Wo had left, the Master said, Yu (Zai Wo) has no humaneness! Only after a child is three years old does he leave the bosom of his father and mother. The three-year mourning period is a custom common to everyone in the world. Surely Yu, too, enjoyed his three years of loving from father and mother!

22   The Master said, Stuff yourself with food all day, never give your mind anything to do, and you're a problem! There's chess, isn't there? There's *weiqi*, isn't there?—wiser at least to busy yourself with these.

23   Zilu said, Does the gentleman esteem courage? The Master said, The gentleman holds rightness in highest esteem. A gentleman who possesses courage but lacks rightness will become rebellious. A petty man who possesses courage but lacks rightness will turn to thievery.

---

11   The three-year mourning period for parents is generally interpreted to mean into the third year—that is, twenty-five or twenty-seven months.

24 Zigong asked, Does the gentleman too have things he hates? The Master said, He has his hates. He hates those who go on about what is hateful in others. He hates those in low position who revile those above them. He hates courage that ignores ritual decorum; he hates firmness and decision that is not open-minded.

Zigong said, I too have things I hate. I hate plagiarists who pretend to be wise. I hate unruly people who pretend to be courageous. I hate scandal mongerers who pretend to be upright.

25 The Master said, Women and petty persons are the hardest to look after. Treat them in a friendly manner, and they become impertinent; keep them at a distance, and they take offense.

26 The Master said, Forty and hated by others—and he'll be so the rest of his life.[12]

---

12 That is, by the age of forty one's character is fixed.

Book Eighteen

1 Weizi left the state; Jizi became a slave; Bi Gan reprimanded him and was killed. Confucius said, The Yin had three who were humane.[1]

2 When Liuxia Hui served as chief judge he was three times dismissed.[2] Someone said, Wouldn't you do better going elsewhere?

Liuxia Hui said, If I apply the Way correctly in serving others, where can I go and not be dismissed three times? And if I applied the Way in a crooked fashion in serving others, what need would I have to leave the country of my father and mother?

3 Duke Jing of Qi, speaking of the treatment that he was prepared to offer Confucius, said, I cannot give him the treatment accorded the senior branch of the Ji family.[3] It would have to be the treatment accorded someone in between the senior and the junior branches. [To Confucius] he said, I'm old—I cannot make proper use of you.

Confucius left the state of Qi.

4 The men of Qi presented Lu with a troupe of women musicians. Ji Huanzi accepted them and for three days failed to appear at court.[4] Confucius left the state.

5 Jie Yu, the madman of Chu, passed by Confucius, singing these words:

---

1 Weizi reprimanded his half-brother Zhou for his evil ways but, his advice unheeded, left the state. When his reprimands were ignored, Jizi, an uncle of Zhou, feigned madness and became a slave. Bi Gan, another uncle of Zhou, was put to death for his remonstrances.

2 On Liuxia Hui, see 15:14.

3 On Duke Jing, see 12:11 and 16:12.

4 The musicians were intended to distract Ji Huanzi from affairs of state and weaken the power of the state of Lu.

Phoenix, phoenix,
how your virtue has ebbed away!
What's past has gone beyond mending
but what's to come is still within reach.
Leave off! Leave off!
Danger waits those who work at governing today!

Confucius got down from his carriage, hoping to speak with him, but the madman ran away and hid, and he was never able to speak to him.

6 Changju and Jieni[5] had teamed up to do the plowing when Confucius passed by. He sent Zilu to ask them where the ford was.

Changju said, Who is that driving the carriage?

That's Kong Qiu, said Zilu.

Kong Qiu of Lu?

Yes, Zilu replied.

Then he must know where the ford is.

Zilu put the same question to Jieni. Jieni said, Who are you?

I'm Zhongyou (Zilu).

Are you a follower of this Kong Qiu of Lu?

I am, Zilu replied.

Turmoil, turmoil, said Jieni—the whole world's that way, and who's going to change it? Rather than following someone who shuns this person or that, wouldn't it be better to follow one who shuns the world itself? Then he went back to breaking up the clods, never stopping.

Zilu returned and reported this to Confucius, who sighed and said, One cannot simply live with the birds and beasts. If I am not to join with my fellow men, who am I to join with? If the Way prevailed in the world, I would not try to change things.

---

5 Long Marsh and Bravely Drowned, fanciful names suggestive of the fictional characters described in the *Zhuangzi*.

7   Zilu was accompanying the Master but had fallen behind when he came upon an old man carrying a pole with a basket dangling from it. Zilu said, Have you seen my Master?

The old man said, Don't know how to move your four limbs, can't tell the five grains apart?[6]—who is your "Master"? Then he stuck the pole in the ground and went to weeding. Zilu folded his hands in a gesture of respect and stood waiting.

The old man put Zilu up for the night, killed a chicken and cooked millet for a meal, and introduced him to his two sons.

The following day, Zilu caught up with Confucius and reported what had happened. The Master said, He's a recluse! and sent Zilu to look for the man again, but when he got to the place, the man was gone.

Zilu said,[7] If you fail to serve the ruler, you lack rightness. You understand that the etiquette between elder and younger cannot be set aside. How, then, can the right relations between ruler and subject be set aside? You want to keep yourselves unsullied, but you bring confusion to a much greater relationship. The gentleman, in serving the ruler, is carrying out his rightful duty. That the Way does not prevail today—we know that already!

8   Those who withdrew from the world: Bo Yi, Shu Qi, Yu Zhong, Yi Yi, Zhu Zhang, Liuxia Hui, Shao Lian.

The Master said, They never lowered their aims, never let themselves be disgraced—that would be Bo Yi and Shu Qi, would it not?

He said, Liuxia Hui and Shao Lian lowered their aims and suffered disgrace. But they spoke in accordance with reason, acted in accordance with careful thought—that much can be said of them.

---

6   The five grains are rice, millet, panicled millet, wheat, and pulse.

7   It is unclear whether Zilu speaks these words to the two sons of the old man or to Confucius. I have translated as though the former were the case. If the latter, the word "you" would have to be changed to "they."

And he said, Yu Zhong and Yi Yi lived in seclusion, gave up speaking, kept themselves free of stain, and in their withdrawal accorded with expediency. I myself differ from these men. I have no hard and fast dos and don'ts.

9 The Grand Music Master Zhi went to Qi; Gan, musician of the second meal, went to Chu; Liao, musician of the third meal, went to Cai; Que, musician of the fourth meal, went to Qin. The drummer Fang Shu went to the Yellow River region. The hand-drum player Wu went to the Han River region. The Lesser Music Master Yang and Xiang, who played the chiming stones, went to the coast.[8]

10 The duke of Zhou said to the duke of Lu, The gentleman does not neglect his relatives and does not cause his high officials to be resentful because he does not heed them. He does not dismiss old associates without good reason, and he does not demand perfection from one person.

11 The Zhou had eight men of station: elder brother Da and elder brother Kuo; middle brother Tu and middle brother Hu; younger brother Ye and younger brother Xia; youngest brother Sui and youngest brother Kuo.[9]

---

8 This describes a dispersal of court musicians in a time of political decline. One theory is that it pertains to the troubled last days of the Yin dynasty; another that it refers to the state of Lu in Confucius's time.

9 That is, four sets of twins, all holding public office, said to be an auspicious sign of the flourishing years of the Zhou dynasty.

Book Nineteen

1 Zizhang said, When a man of station spies danger, he is prepared to give his life.[1] When he spies gain, he thinks of what is right. At a sacrifice, he thinks of respectfulness; at a funeral, he thinks of grief. If he does this much, he will get by.

2 Zizhang said, He adheres to virtue but not expansively; he trusts in the Way but not with conviction—how can you tell if he's really there or not?

3 A disciple of Zixia asked Zizhang about personal relations. Zizhang said, What does Zixia say? The disciple replied, Zixia says, Associate with those who are fit to be associated with; reject those who are not.

Zizhang said, That's different from what I've heard. The gentleman honors worthy persons and tolerates the multitude. He applauds good men and sympathizes with those who lack ability. Am I myself a person of great worth? If so, why shouldn't I tolerate others? Am I a person who lacks worth? If so, others will reject me. What need is there for me to reject others?

4 Zixia said, Although it may be a lesser Way, it must have things worth noting. But if pursued too far, there's a danger of becoming mired in it—therefore, the gentleman does not do so.

5 Zixia said, Day by day understanding what is beyond you, month by month never forgetting what you *can* do—you may be called a lover of learning.

6 Zixia said, Broad in learning, dedicated in will, acute in questioning, reflecting on things close at hand—look for humaneness there.

---

1 Presumably, danger to the state.

7 Zixia said, The hundred craftsmen stay in their workshops in order to accomplish their tasks. The gentleman studies in order to perfect his Way.

8 Zixia said, When the petty man makes a mistake, he invariably tries to gloss it over.[2]

9 Zixia said, The gentleman has three changes of appearance. Seen from a distance, he is austere. Approach more closely, and he is mild. Listen to his words, and he is sharp-spoken.

10 Zixia said, The gentleman must be trusted before he can demand labor from the common people. If he is not trusted, they will think he is being harsh with them. He must be trusted before he can remonstrate [with his superiors]. If he is not trusted, they will think he is speaking ill of them.

11 Zixia said, If in regard to the major virtues you do not overstep the line, in regard to the minor virtues you may be permitted a little coming and going.

12 Ziyou said, The young men who are followers of Zixia are competent at sprinkling and sweeping, receiving and responding to guests, advancing and retiring. But these are minor affairs. Question them on fundamentals, and they have no answer. How can that be?

When Zixia heard this, he said, Ah—Ziyou is mistaken. In the Way of the gentleman, what is to be taught first, what can be put aside until later? It's like the case of plants or trees, which require different types of handling. But the Way of the gentleman—how can it be handled incorrectly? And who understands it from beginning to end?—only the sage can do that!

13 Zixia said, Hold public office, and if you have time left over, study. Study, and if you have time left over, hold public office.

---

2 See 1:8.

14 Ziyou said, In mourning, if grief is fully expressed, stop there.

15 Ziyou said, My friend Zizhang can do difficult things, but he has not yet mastered humaneness.

16 Master Zeng said, Zizhang is imposing indeed, but side by side with one like that it's hard to achieve humaneness.

17 Master Zeng said, I have heard our Master say, People never fully express what is in them. If one had to cite an exception, it would be when they are mourning a parent.

18 Master Zeng said, I have heard our Master say, The filial piety displayed by Meng Zhuang Zi can be matched in other respects. But the way he refrained from dismissing the officials appointed by his father or departing from his father's ways of governing—that would be hard to match.

19 The Meng family appointed Yang Fu to the post of chief judge, and he questioned Master Zeng about the office.

   Master Zeng said, Those in high places have lost the Way, and the common people have long been without guidance. When you uncover the facts of a case, be sorrowful and compassionate, never pleased with yourself.

20 Zigong said, Zhou was not really as evil as they say. That is why the gentleman hates to be held in low esteem—all the evil in the world ends up on him.

21 Zigong said, The gentleman's errors are like eclipses of the sun or moon. His errors can be seen by all, and when he corrects them, all look up in admiration.

22 Gongsun Chao of Wei questioned Zigong, saying, Where did Zhongni (Confucius) study?

   Zigong said, The Way of Wen and Wu has not yet disappeared completely. Among the populace, worthy men remember the essentials, and those of little worth remember the minor points. There are none who do not possess the Way of Wen and Wu, so how could our Master fail to study it? But how can you say he studied with any particular teacher?

23 Shusun Wushu, speaking to the high officials at court, said, Zigong is a worthier man than Zhongni. Zifu Jingbo reported this to Zigong.

Zigong said, To use the simile of the wall surrounding a building, my wall is only shoulder-high, so you can get a good view of the living quarters inside. But Confucius's wall is many feet high. Unless you enter by the gate, you can never see the beauty of the ancestral altar or the wealth of rooms for the hundred officials. And those who manage to enter that gate are likely to be few. So it's not surprising that that gentleman said what he did.

24 When Shusun Wushu spoke disparagingly of Zhongni, Zigong said, There's no point in that. You can't speak disparagingly of Zhongni. The worth of other persons is like a hill or knoll—you can still walk over it. But Zhongni is like the sun or the moon—no one can walk over them. Someone may decide to break off relations with the sun and moon, but what difference does that make to them? It only shows how little he understands his own capacity.

25 Chen Ziqin said to Zigong, You are being too modest. How could Zhongni be a worthier man than you?

Zigong said, The gentleman speaks one word and shows that he is wise, speaks one word and shows that he is unwise. Therefore, he must be careful how he speaks. Our Master can no more be equaled than one can mount a stairway to the sky. If our Master were to preside over a state or a powerful family, then, as the saying has it, If he raised them, they would stand; if he led, they would go forward; if he chose peace, they would flock around; if he moved, they would move in harmony. In life he is glorious; in death, deeply mourned. How, then, could he be equaled?

Book Twenty

1 Yao said, Ah, you, Shun—the destiny decreed by Heaven rests with you. Hold sincerely to the center. If those within the four seas suffer hardship and want, Heaven's bounty will end forever.

And Shun voiced the same command [when he ceded the throne] to Yu.

[Tang] said, I, the little one, Lu, venture to sacrifice this black ox, I venture to report clearly to the most august Lord above. The guilty one I have not ventured to pardon, but I do nothing to hinder the Lord's officials. May they be chosen in accordance with the Lord's will. If there is blame on my part, let the ten thousand regions not suffer. If the ten thousand regions have any blame, let that blame rest on me.

Zhou has received great gifts; good persons are enriched. Although Zhou has kinsmen, they cannot equal persons of humaneness. If the people have any fault, may the blame be upon me alone.[1]

2 Carefully adjust the weights and measures; clarify the laws and regulations; restore offices that have been discontinued—then the governing of the four directions will proceed. Reestablish states that have been wiped out; appoint heirs to successions that have come to an end; promote men who have gone into hiding—then the people of the empire will give their hearts to you. What is to be held in esteem: the people, food, mourning, and sacrifice.[2]

---

1   The statements in this passage are couched in the archaic style typical of the *Book of Documents*, though no exact parallels are found in the present text of that work. The first purports to be the words of the sage ruler Yao when he ceded the throne to Shun and repeated by Shun when he ceded it to Yu, the founder of the Xia dynasty. This is followed by a speech by Tang, who overthrew the evil last ruler of the Xia and founded the Yin dynasty. The third section presumably represents the words of King Wu, who overthrew the evil last ruler of the Yin and founded the Zhou dynasty.

2   This and the following passage are often taken to be a continuation of the preceding passage and interpreted as describing the actions of the founders of the Zhou dynasty.

3   Be tolerant, and you win over the multitude. Be trustworthy, and the people will trust you. Be diligent, and your work will go well. Be fair, and the people will rejoice.

4   Zizhang questioned Confucius about government, saying, How should one proceed in order to govern effectively?

The Master said, Honor the five desirables, avoid the four evils—then you can govern effectively.

Zizhang said, What are the five desirables?

The Master said, The gentleman is bountiful but not extravagant, exacts labor but rouses no resentment, has desires but is not covetous, is self-possessed but not arrogant, dignified but not oppressively so.

Zizhang said, What do you mean by bountiful but not extravagant?

The Master said, In bestowing benefit, go by what benefits the people—is this not what is meant by bountiful but not extravagant? Select those appropriate for the task and exact labor from them—then who can feel resentment? Desire humaneness, and you will achieve humaneness—how can you be called covetous? The gentleman does not discriminate between the many and the few, the little and the big, and would never be overbearing—is this not what is meant by self-possessed but not arrogant? The gentleman straightens his clothing and cap and is careful how he looks at others, so that just viewing him from a distance, people are impressed—is this not what is meant by dignified but not oppressively so?

Zizhang said, What are the four evils?

The Master said, To execute people without first instructing them—this is called tyranny. To demand to see results without first giving warning—this is called unreasonableness. To be lax in issuing orders and then suddenly call for results—this is called brigandage. When something has to be allotted anyway,

to be stingy in allotting it—this is called the habit of government clerks.

5 Confucius said, If you do not understand the will of Heaven, you will have no way to become a gentleman. If you do not understand ritual, you will have nowhere to take your stand. If you do not understand words, you will have no way to know people.

Glossary of Persons and Places

AO Legendary, rowdy strong man of antiquity who met a violent end [14:6].

BI Town in the state of Lu controlled by the Ji family [6:9, 11:25, 16:1, 17:5].

BI GAN Uncle of Zhou, last ruler of the Yin dynasty, who was killed by Zhou because of his remonstrances [18:1].

BI XI Identity uncertain; started a revolution in Zhongmou in an area controlled by the state of Jin [17:7].

BO Family of the state of Qi [14:10].

BO YI AND SHU QI Sons of the ruler of a small state in Yin times. Their father intended the younger, Shu Qi, to succeed him, but Shu Qi deferred to Bo Yi and both brothers left the state. When King Wu overthrew the Yin dynasty, they admonished him for his violence, withdrew to Mount Shouyang, and died there of starvation [5:23, 7:14, 16:12, 18:8].

BONIU *See* Ran Boniu.

BOOK OF CHANGES (YIJING) Early text on divination, one of the Confucian Classics [7:16, 13:22].

BOOK OF DOCUMENTS (SHUJING, OR *CLASSIC OF HISTORY)* Collection of historical documents pertaining to ancient times, one of the Confucian Classics [2:21, 7:17, 14:42, 20:1].

BOOK OF ODES (SHIJING, OR *CLASSIC OF POETRY)* Collection of poems of ancient times, one of the Confucian Classics [1:15, 2:2, 3:2, 3:20, 7:17, 8:3, 8:8, 9:15, 9:28, 9:32, 11:6, 12:10, 13:5, 14:41, 15:11, 16:13, 17:9, 17:10, 17:18].

BOQIN Son of the duke of Zhou and first ruler of the state of Lu [18:10].

BOYU Personal name Li; son of Confucius [16:13, 17:10].

CAI   Small state to the southwest of Lu visited by Confucius [11:2, 18:9].

CHAI   *See* Zigao.

CHANGJU   Farmer recluse [18:6].

CHE   Grandson of Duke Ling of Wei [7:14].

CHEN   Ministerial family of the state of Qi; identical to Tian [14:22].

CHEN   Small state to the southwest of Lu visited by Confucius [5:22, 7:30, 11:2, 15:2].

CHEN CHENGZI   Official of the state of Qi who assassinated Duke Jian of Qi in 481 B.C.E. [14:22].

CHEN GANG   *See* Ziqin.

CHEN HENG   *See* Chen Chengzi.

CHEN WEN ZI   Official of the state of Qi [5:19].

CHEN ZIQIN   Perhaps identical to Ziqin [19:25].

CHI   *See* Gongxi Zihua.

CHU   Large and important state in the Yangzi Valley [5:19, 13:16, 18:5, 18:9].

CONFUCIUS (551–479 B.C.E.)   Latinized form of Kong fuzi, or Respected Master Kong; family name Kong, personal name Qiu, polite name Zhongni; often referred to simply as Zi, or the Master.

CUI ZI   Official of the state of Qi who assassinated Duke Zhuang of Qi in 548 B.C.E. [5:19].

DAN   *See* Duke of Zhou.

DAXIANG   Village [9:2].

DENG   Small state to the south of Lu [14:12].

DI   Non-Chinese people who lived to the northwest of China [3:5, 13:19].

DOCUMENTS   See *Book of Documents*.

DUKE AI   Ruler of the state of Lu (494–468 B.C.E.) when power was in the hands of the Ji family [2:19, 3:21, 6:3, 12:9, 14:22].

DUKE DING   Ruler of the state of Lu (509–495 B.C.E.) [3:19, 13:15].

DUKE HUAN OF LU   Ruler of the state of Lu and ancestor of the three branches of the Ji family [16:3].

DUKE HUAN OF QI   Illustrious ruler of the state of Qi (685–643 B.C.E.) [14:16–14:18].

DUKE JIAN OF QI   Ruler of the state of Qi (484–481 B.C.E.) who was assassinated by Chen Chengzi [14:22].

DUKE JING OF QI   Ruler of the state of Qi (547–490 B.C.E.) [12:11, 16:12, 18:3].

DUKE LING OF WEI   Ruler of the state of Wei (534–493 B.C.E.) [6:28, 7:14, 14:20, 15:1].

DUKE OF LU   *See* Boqin.

DUKE OF ZHOU   Personal name Dan; younger brother of King Wu, founder of the Zhou dynasty, who was enfeoffed as the ruler of the state of Lu [3:15, 7:5, 8:11, 11:17, 13:7, 18:10].

DUKE WEN OF JIN   Illustrious ruler of the state of Jin (636–628 B.C.E.) [14:16].

DUKE ZHAO   Ruler of the state of Lu (541–509 B.C.E.) [7:30].

FAN CHI   Disciple of Confucius [2:5, 6:22, 12:21, 12:22, 13:4, 13:19].

FAN XU   *See* Fan Chi.

FANG SHU   Drummer [18:9].

GAN   Musician [18:9].

GAO CHAI   *See* Zigao.

GAO YAO   Minister to the sage ruler Shun [12:22].

GAO ZONG   Sage ruler of the Yin dynasty [14:42].

GONGBO LIAO   Identity uncertain [14:38].

GONGMING JIA   Identity unknown [14:14].

GONGSHAN FURAO   Retainer of the Ji family in the state of Lu who started a revolution in the region of Bi against the family in 502 B.C.E. [17:5].

GONGSHU WENZI   Official of the state of Wei, considerably older than Confucius [5:15, 14:14, 14:19, 14:20].

GONGSUN CHAO   Official of the state of Wei [19:22].

GONGXI HUA   *See* Gongxi Zihua.

GONGXI ZIHUA   Personal name Chi; disciple of Confucius [5:8, 6:4, 7:33, 11:26].

GONGYE CHANG   Son-in-law of Confucius [5:1].

GRAND MUSIC MASTER OF LU   [3:23].

GRAND MUSIC MASTER ZHI   [8:15, 18:9].

GUAN ZHONG   Famous official under Duke Huan of Qi [3:22, 14:10, 14:17, 14:18].

HAN   Hand-drum player [18:9].

HU   Village whose location is uncertain [7:28].

HUAN TUI   Minister of war in the state of Song who threatened to kill Confucius [7:22].

HUI   *See* Yan Yuan.

INVOCATOR TUO   Noted for his eloquence [6:16, 14:20].

JI   Ancestor of the founders of the Zhou dynasty [14:6].

JI   Three ministerial families of the states of Lu and Wu descended from Duke Huan of Lu [3:1, 3:2, 3:6, 6:9, 7:30, 11:17, 12:2, 13:2, 14:22, 14:38, 16:1, 16:3, 17:1, 18:3].

JI HUANZI   Father of Ji Kangzi and head of the most important branch of the Ji family (505–492 B.C.E.) [18:4].

JI KANGZI   Head of the Ji family (492–468 B.C.E.) [2:20, 6:8, 10:12, 11:7, 12:17–12:19, 14:20].

JI LI   *See* King Wen.

JI SUN   *See* Ji Wen Zi.

JI WEN ZI (D. 568 B.C.E.)   Posthumous name of Ji Sun Xingfu of the Ji family of Lu [5:20, 14:38].

JI ZICHENG   Official of the state of Wei? [12:8].

JI ZIRAN   Member of the Ji family of Lu? [11:24].

JIE YU   Madman in the state of Chu [18:5].

JIENI   Farmer recluse [18:6].

JILU   *See* Zilu.

JIN   Powerful state in northeastern China [17:7].

JING OF WEI   Ducal son of Wei [13:8].

JIU   Ducal son of Qi who was killed on orders from his brother, Duke Huan of Qi [14:17, 14:18].

JIZI, VISCOUNT OF JI   Uncle of Zhou, last ruler of the Yin dynasty [18:1].

JUFU   Town in the state of Lu [13:17].

KANGSHU   Younger brother of the duke of Zhou who was enfeoffed as the ruler of the state of Wei [13:7].

KING WEN   Father of King Wu, founder of the Zhou dynasty [19:22].

KING WU   Founder of the Zhou dynasty. Confucius regarded him and his father, King Wen, as the creators of Zhou culture [8:20, 13:7, 19:22, 20:1].

KONG QIU   *See* Confucius.

KONG WENZI   *See* Gongshu Wenzi.

KUAI KUI   Son of Duke Ling of Wei [7:14].

KUANG   Town whose inhabitants threatened Confucius [9:5, 11:23].

LAO   Identity unknown [9:7].

LESSER MUSIC MASTER YANG   [18:9].

LI   *See* Boyu.

LIAO   Musician [18:9].

LIN FANG   Disciple of Confucius? [3:4, 3:6].

LIUXIA HUI   Official of the state of Lu before the time of Confucius who was much esteemed in the Confucian school [15:14, 18:2, 18:8].

LORD OF SHE   *See* Shen Juliang.

LU   *See* Tang.

LU   Small state in northeastern China that was the native state of Confucius [13:7].

MAN   Non-Chinese people who lived to the south of China [15:6].

MASTER RAN   *See* Ran You.

MASTER YOU   *See* You Ruo.

MASTER ZENG   Prominent disciple of Confucius [1:4, 1:9, 4:15, 8:3–8:7, 11:18, 12:24, 14:28, 19:17–19:19].

MENG   Senior branch of the Ji family of Lu [19:19].

MENG GONGCHUO   Member of the senior branch of the Ji family of Lu [14:12, 14:13].

MENG JING ZI   Son of Meng Wu Bo and official of the state of Lu [8:4].

MENG WU BO   Son of Meng Yi Zi and official of the state of Lu [2:6, 5:8].

MENG YI ZI   Official of the state of Lu [2:5].

MENG ZHIFAN   Official of the state of Lu [6:15].

MENG ZHUANG ZI (D. 550 B.C.E.)   Distinguished official of the state of Lu [19:18].

MIN ZIQIAN   Disciple of Confucius [6:9, 11:3, 11:5, 11:13, 11:14].

MO   Non-Chinese people who lived to the north of China [15:6].

MOUNT DONGMENG   Mountain in the Zhuanyu area of the state of Lu [16:1].

MOUNT SHOUYANG   Mountain whose location is unknown [16:12].

MOUNT TAI   Sacred mountain in the state of Qi [3:6].

MUSIC MASTER MIAN   [15:42].

NAN RONG   Disciple of Confucius, perhaps identical to Nangong Kuo [5:2, 11:6].

NANGONG KUO   Identity uncertain [14:6].

NANZI   Wife of Duke Ling of Wei [6:28].

NING WU ZI   Official of the state of Wei [5:21].

ODES   See *Book of Odes.*

OLD PENG   Identity uncertain; perhaps a long-lived sage of antiquity [7:1].

PI CHEN   Eminent official of the state of Zheng in the generation before that of Confucius [14:9].

PIAN   Village in the state of Qi [14:10].

QI   Famous horse [14:35].

QI   Large and powerful state to the north of Lu [6:4, 7:13, 17:1, 18:3, 18:4, 18:9].

QI   (written with a different character from the name of the large state) Small state where descendants of the ruling family of the Xia dynasty were enfeoffed [3:9].

QIDIAO KAI   Disciple of Confucius [5:6].

QIN   State in far western China [18:9].

QIU   *See* Confucius.

QIU   *See* Ran You.

QU BOYU   High official of the state of Wei [14:26, 15:7].

QUE   Musician [18:9].

QUE   Village in the state of Lu [14:46].

RAN BONIU   Disciple of Confucius [6:10, 11:3].

RAN QIU   *See* Ran You.

RAN YOU   Disciple of Confucius in service to the Ji family [3:6, 5:8, 6:4, 6:8, 6:12, 7:14, 11:3, 11:13, 11:17, 11:22, 11:24, 11:26, 13:9, 13:14, 14:13, 16:1].

RU BEI   Identity uncertain [17:20].

SHANG   *See* Zixia.

SHAO HU   Supporter of the ducal son Jiu of Qi who died when Jiu was killed on orders from Duke Huan of Qi [14:17].

SHAO LIAN   Recluse? [18:8].

SHEN   *See* Master Zeng.

SHEN CHENG   Identity uncertain [5:11].

SHEN JULIANG   Lord or governor of the region of She and official of the state of Chu [7:18, 13:16, 13:18].

SHI   *See* Zizhang.

SHI SHU   Eminent official of the state of Zheng in the generation before that of Confucius [14:9].

SHI YU   Distinguished official of the state of Wei [15:7].

SHUN   Sage ruler of antiquity who ceded the throne to Yu, founder of the Xia dynasty [6:30, 8:18, 8:20, 12:22, 14:44, 15:5, 20:1].

SHUSUN WUSHU   Official of the state of Lu, some years younger than Confucius [19:23, 19:24].

SI   *See* Zigong.

SIMA NIU   Brother of Huan Tui [12:3–12:5].

SONG   Small state to the south of Lu where descendants of the ruling family of the Yin dynasty were enfeoffed [3:9, 7:22].

SONG ZHAO   Prince of the state of Song who was noted for his good looks [6:16].

STONE GATE   Outer gate of the Lu capital [14:40].

TAI BO   Eldest brother of Ji Li, King Wen of Zhou. Knowing that his father wished to make Ji Li his heir, Tai Bo left the area of the Zhou people and settled on the coast in a region inhabited by non-Chinese tribes and founded the state of Wu. What Confucius means by "three times he relinquished the right to the empire" is unknown [8:1].

TANG   Personal name Lu; founder of the Yin dynasty [20:1].

TANG   *See* Yao.

TANG   Dynasty ruled by Yao [12:22].

TANTAI MIEMING   Identity unknown [6:14].

TIAN   Ministerial family of the state of Qi; identical to Chen [14:22].

WANGSUN JIA   Official of the state of Wei [3:13, 14:20].

WEI   Small state immediately to the west of Lu [9:15: 13:3, 13:7, 13:9, 14:26, 14:41, 15:1, 19:22].

WEISHENG GAO   Identity uncertain [5:24].

WEISHENG MU   Identity unknown [14:34].

WEIZI, VISCOUNT OF WEI   Half-brother of Zhou, last ruler of the Yin dynasty [18:1].

WU   Hand-drum player [18:9].

WU   Small state on the seacoast ruled by a family with the same Ji surname as the ruling family of Lu [7:30, 9:6].

WU MENGZI   Wife of Duke Zhao of Lu [7:30].

WUCHENG   Town in the state of Lu [6:14, 17:4].

WUMA QI   Identity uncertain; perhaps a disciple of Confucius or a member of his circle [7:30].

XIAN   *See* Yuan Si.

XIANG   Chiming-stones player [18:9].

XUE   Small state near Lu [14:12].

YAN LU   Father of Yan Yuan [11:8].

YAN PINGZHONG   Distinguished official of the state of Qi [5:17].

YAN YING   *See* Yan Pingzhong.

YAN YUAN   Personal name Hui; distinguished disciple of Confucius who died young [5:26, 6:7, 6:11, 7:10, 8:5, 9:11, 9:20–9:22, 11:3, 11:4, 11:7–11:11, 11:19, 11:23, 12:1, 15:11].

YANG FU   Chief judge of the state of Lu [19:19].

YANG HU   Military leader and official in service to the Ji family who led a revolt and was forced to flee to the state of Qi [9:5, 17:1, 17:5].

YANG HUO   Usually regarded as identical to Yang Hu [17:1].

YAO   Sage ruler of antiquity who ceded the throne to Shun [6:30, 8:19, 14:44, 20:1].

YI   Legendary, rowdy archer of antiquity who met a violent end [14:6].

YI   Non-Chinese people who lived to the east of China [3:5, 13:19].

YI   Area in the state of Wei [3:24].

YI YI   Recluse [18:8].

YI YIN   Minister who assisted Tang, founder of the Yin dynasty [12:22].

YONG   *See* Zhonggong Ran Yong.

YOU   *See* Zilu.

YOU RUO   Disciple of Confucius [1:2, 1:12, 1:13, 12:9].

YU   Sage ruler, successor to Shun, and founder of the Xia dynasty. He is associated with flood control and encouragement of agriculture [8:18, 8:20, 8:21, 14:6, 20:1].

YU   *See* Shun.

YU ZHONG   Younger brother of Tai Bo [18:8].

YUAN RANG   Old friend of Confucius [14:45].

YUAN SI   Disciple of Confucius [6:5, 14:1, 14:2].

ZAI WO   Disciple of Confucius [3:21, 5:10, 6:26, 11:3, 17:21].

ZAI YU   *See* Zai Wo.

ZANG WENZHONG (D. 617 B.C.E.)   Prime minister of the state of Lu [5:18, 14:13, 15:14].

ZANG WUZHONG   Grandson of Zang Wenzhong and official of the state of Lu [14:15].

ZENG CAN   *See* Master Zeng.

ZENG SHEN   *See* Master Zeng.

ZENG XI   Father of Zeng Shen [11:26].

ZHAO   Powerful family of the state of Jin [14:12].

ZHENG   Small state to the west of Lu [14:9, 15:11, 17:18].

ZHONGGONG RAN YONG   Disciple of Confucius [6:6, 12:2, 13:2].

ZHONGMOU   Area controlled by the state of Jin [17:7].

ZHONGNI   *See* Confucius.

ZHONGSHU YU   *See* Gongshu Wenzi.

ZHONGYOU   *See* Zilu.

ZHOU   (written with a different character from the name of the dynasty) Last ruler of the Yin dynasty who is depicted in legend as a tyrant [18:1, 19:20].

ZHOU REN   Wise man of antiquity [16:1].

ZHU ZHANG   Recluse [18:8].

ZHUAN   Official of the state of Wei [14:19].

ZHUANGZI OF PIAN   Noted for his valor [14:13].

ZHUANYU   Small feudal domain in the state of Lu [16:1].

ZICHAN OF DONGLI   Prime minister of the state of Zheng in the generation before that of Confucius who was much admired by Confucius [5:16, 14:9, 14:10].

ZIFU JINGBO   Official in service to the Ji family [14:38, 19:23].

ZIGAO   Disciple of Confucius and steward of Bi [11:18, 11:25].

ZIGONG   Personal name Si; prominent disciple of Confucius [1:10, 1:15, 2:13, 3:17, 5:4, 5:9, 5:13, 5:15, 6:8, 6:30, 7:14, 9:6, 9:13, 11:3, 11:13, 11:16, 11:19, 12:7, 12:8, 12:23, 13:20, 13:24, 14:18, 14:30, 14:31, 14:37, 15:3, 15:10, 15:24, 17:19, 17:24, 19:20–19:25].

ZIHUA   *See* Gongxi Zihua.

ZIJIAN   Disciple of Confucius [5:3].

ZILU   Personal name You; prominent disciple of Confucius. Steward to the Ji family, later in service to the ruler of the state of Wei, he died while fighting in Wei in 480 B.C.E. [2:17, 5:7, 5:8, 5:14, 5:26, 6:8, 6:28, 7:10, 7:18, 7:34, 9:12, 9:27, 9:28, 10:22, 11:13, 11:15, 11:18, 11:22, 11:24, 11:25, 11:26, 12:12, 13:1, 13:3, 13:28, 14:13, 14:17, 14:23, 14:38, 14:40, 14:44, 15:2, 15:4, 16:1, 17:5, 17:7, 17:8, 17:23, 18:6, 18:7].

ZIQIN   Disciple of Confucius [1:10, 16:13].

ZISANG BOZI   Identity unknown [6:2].

ZIXI   Official of the state of Chu [14:10].

ZIXIA   Personal name Shang; prominent disciple of Confucius [1:7, 2:8, 3:8, 6:13, 11:3, 11:16, 12:5, 12:22, 13:17, 19:3–19:13].

ZIYOU   Disciple of Confucius and steward of Wucheng [2:7, 4:26, 6:14, 11:3, 17:4, 19:12, 19:14, 19:15].

ZIYU   Eminent official of the state of Zheng in the generation before that of Confucius [14:9].

ZIWEN   Prime minister of the state of Chu [5:19].

ZIZHANG   Personal name Shi; prominent disciple of Confucius [2:18, 2:23, 5:19, 11:16, 11:18, 11:20, 12:6, 12:10, 12:14, 12:20, 14:42, 15:6, 15:42, 17:6, 19:1–19:3, 19:15, 19:16, 20:4].

ZOU   Birthplace of the father of Confucius [3:15].

ZUOQIU MING   Identity uncertain [5:25].

Other Works in the
Columbia Asian Studies Series

Essays in Idleness: The Tsurezuregusa of Kenkō, tr. Donald Keene. Also in paperback ed. 1967

The Pillow Book of Sei Shōnagon, tr. Ivan Morris, 2 vols. 1967

Two Plays of Ancient India: The Little Clay Cart and the Minister's Seal, tr. J. A. B. van Buitenen 1968

The Complete Works of Chuang Tzu, tr. Burton Watson 1968

The Romance of the Western Chamber (Hsi Hsiang chi), tr. S. I. Hsiung. Also in paperback ed. 1968

The Manyōshū, Nippon Gakujutsu Shinkōkai edition. Paperback ed. only. 1969

Records of the Historian: Chapters from the Shih chi of Ssu-ma Ch'ien, tr. Burton Watson. Paperback ed. only. 1969

Cold Mountain: 100 Poems by the T'ang Poet Han-shan, tr. Burton Watson. Also in paperback ed. 1970

Twenty Plays of the Nō Theatre, ed. Donald Keene. Also in paperback ed. 1970

Chūshingura: The Treasury of Loyal Retainers, tr. Donald Keene. Also in paperback ed. 1971; rev. ed. 1997

The Zen Master Hakuin: Selected Writings, tr. Philip B. Yampolsky 1971

Chinese Rhyme-Prose: Poems in the Fu Form from the Han and Six Dynasties Periods, tr. Burton Watson. Also in paperback ed. 1971

Kūkai: Major Works, tr. Yoshito S. Hakeda. Also in paperback ed. 1972

The Old Man Who Does as He Pleases: Selections from the Poetry and Prose of Lu Yu, tr. Burton Watson 1973

The Lion's Roar of Queen Śrīmālā, tr. Alex and Hideko Wayman 1974

Courtier and Commoner in Ancient China: Selections from the History of the Former Han by Pan Ku, tr. Burton Watson. Also in paperback ed. 1974

Japanese Literature in Chinese, vol. 1: *Poetry and Prose in Chinese by Japanese Writers of the Early Period,* tr. Burton Watson 1975

Japanese Literature in Chinese, vol. 2: *Poetry and Prose in Chinese by Japanese Writers of the Later Period,* tr. Burton Watson 1976

Scripture of the Lotus Blossom of the Fine Dharma, tr. Leon Hurvitz. Also in paperback ed. 1976

Love Song of the Dark Lord: Jayadeva's Gītagovinda, tr. Barbara Stoler Miller. Also in paperback ed. Cloth ed. includes critical text of the Sanskrit. 1977; rev. ed. 1997

Ryōkan: Zen Monk-Poet of Japan, tr. Burton Watson 1977

Calming the Mind and Discerning the Real: From the Lam rim chen mo of Tsoṇ-kha-pa, tr. Alex Wayman 1978

The Hermit and the Love-Thief: Sanskrit Poems of Bhartrihari and Bilhaṇa, tr. Barbara Stoler Miller 1978

The Lute: Kao Ming's P'i-p'a chi, tr. Jean Mulligan. Also in paperback ed. 1980

A Chronicle of Gods and Sovereigns: Jinnō Shōtōki of Kitabatake Chikafusa, tr. H. Paul Varley 1980

Among the Flowers: The Hua-chien chi, tr. Lois Fusek 1982

Grass Hill: Poems and Prose by the Japanese Monk Gensei, tr. Burton Watson 1983

Doctors, Diviners, and Magicians of Ancient China: Biographies of Fang-shih, tr. Kenneth J. DeWoskin. Also in paperback ed. 1983

Theater of Memory: The Plays of Kālidāsa, ed. Barbara Stoler Miller. Also in paperback ed. 1984

The Columbia Book of Chinese Poetry: From Early Times to the Thirteenth Century, ed. and tr. Burton Watson. Also in paperback ed. 1984

Poems of Love and War: From the Eight Anthologies and the Ten Long Poems of Classical Tamil, tr. A. K. Ramanujan. Also in paperback ed. 1985

The Bhagavad Gita: Krishna's Counsel in Time of War, tr. Barbara Stoler Miller 1986

The Columbia Book of Later Chinese Poetry, ed. and tr. Jonathan Chaves. Also in paperback ed. 1986

The Tso Chuan: Selections from China's Oldest Narrative History, tr. Burton Watson 1989

Waiting for the Wind: Thirty-six Poets of Japan's Late Medieval Age, tr. Steven Carter 1989

Selected Writings of Nichiren, ed. Philip B. Yampolsky 1990

Saigyō, Poems of a Mountain Home, tr. Burton Watson 1990

The Book of Lieh Tẓu: A Classic of the Tao, tr. A. C. Graham. Morningside ed. 1990

The Tale of an Anklet: An Epic of South India—The Cilappatikāram of Iḷaṇkō Aṭikaḷ, tr. R. Parthasarathy 1993

Waiting for the Dawn: A Plan for the Prince, tr. with introduction by Wm. Theodore de Bary 1993

Yoshitsune and the Thousand Cherry Trees: A Masterpiece of the Eighteenth-Century Japanese Puppet Theater, tr., annotated, and with introduction by Stanleigh H. Jones, Jr. 1993

The Lotus Sutra, tr. Burton Watson. Also in paperback ed. 1993

The Classic of Changes: A New Translation of the I Ching *as Interpreted by Wang Bi*, tr. Richard John Lynn 1994

Beyond Spring: Tз'u Poems of the Sung Dynasty, tr. Julie Landau 1994

The Columbia Anthology of Traditional Chinese Literature, ed. Victor H. Mair 1994

Scenes for Mandarins: The Elite Theater of the Ming, tr. Cyril Birch 1995

Letters of Nichiren, ed. Philip B. Yampolsky; tr. Burton Watson et al. 1996

Unforgotten Dreams: Poems by the Zen Monk Shōtetsu, tr. Steven D. Carter 1997

The Vimalakirti Sutra, tr. Burton Watson 1997

Japanese and Chinese Poems to Sing: The Wakan rōei shū, tr. J. Thomas Rimer and Jonathan Chaves 1997

Breeze Through Bamboo: Kanshi of Ema Saikō, tr. Hiroaki Sato 1998

A Tower for the Summer Heat, by Li Yu, tr. Patrick Hanan 1998

Traditional Japanese Theater: An Anthology of Plays, by Karen Brazell 1998

The Original Analects: Sayings of Confucius and His Successors (0479–0249), by E. Bruce Brooks and A. Taeko Brooks 1998

The Classic of the Way and Virtue: A New Translation of the Tao-te ching *of Laoзi as Interpreted by Wang Bi*, tr. Richard John Lynn 1999

The Four Hundred Songs of War and Wisdom: An Anthology of Poems from Classical Tamil, The Puṟanāṉūṟu, ed. and tr. George L. Hart and Hank Heifetz 1999

Original Tao: Inward Training (Nei-yeh) *and the Foundations of Taoist Mysticism*, by Harold D. Roth 1999

Lao Tзu's Tao Te Ching: *A Translation of the Startling New Documents Found at Guodian*, by Robert G. Henricks 2000

The Shorter Columbia Anthology of Traditional Chinese Literature, ed. Victor H. Mair 2000

Mistress and Maid (Jiaohongji), by Meng Chengshun, tr. Cyril Birch 2001

Chikamatsu: Five Late Plays, tr. and ed. C. Andrew Gerstle 2001

The Essential Lotus: Selections from the Lotus Sutra, tr. Burton Watson 2002

Early Modern Japanese Literature: An Anthology, 1600–1900, ed. Haruo Shirane 2002

The Sound of the Kiss, or The Story That Must Never Be Told: Pingali Suranna's Kalapurnodayamu, tr. Vecheru Narayana Rao and David Shulman 2003

The Selected Poems of Du Fu, tr. Burton Watson 2003

Far Beyond the Field: Haiku by Japanese Women, tr. Makoto Ueda 2003

Just Living: Poems and Prose by the Japanese Monk Tonna, ed. and tr. Steven D. Carter 2003

Han Feizi: Basic Writings, tr. Burton Watson 2003

Mozi: Basic Writings, tr. Burton Watson 2003

Xunzi: Basic Writings, tr. Burton Watson 2003

Zhuangzi: Basic Writings, tr. Burton Watson 2003

The Awakening of Faith, Attributed to Aśvaghosha, tr. Yoshito S. Hakeda, introduction by Ryuichi Abe 2005

The Tales of the Heike, tr. Burton Watson, ed. Haruo Shirane 2006

Tales of Moonlight and Rain, by Ueda Akinari, tr. with introduction by Anthony H. Chambers 2007

Traditional Japanese Literature: An Anthology, Beginnings to 1600, ed. Haruo Shirane 2007

The Philosophy of Qi, by Kaibara Ekken, tr. Mary Evelyn Tucker 2007

MODERN ASIAN LITERATURE

Modern Japanese Drama: An Anthology, ed. and tr. Ted. Takaya. Also in paperback ed. 1979

Mask and Sword: Two Plays for the Contemporary Japanese Theater, by Yamazaki Masakazu, tr. J. Thomas Rimer 1980

Yokomitsu Riichi, Modernist, by Dennis Keene 1980

Nepali Visions, Nepali Dreams: The Poetry of Laxmiprasad Devkota, tr. David Rubin 1980

Literature of the Hundred Flowers, vol. 1: *Criticism and Polemics,* ed. Hualing Nieh 1981

Literature of the Hundred Flowers, vol. 2: *Poetry and Fiction,* ed. Hualing Nieh 1981

Modern Chinese Stories and Novellas, 1919–1949, ed. Joseph S. M. Lau, C. T. Hsia, and Leo Ou-fan Lee. Also in paperback ed. 1984

A View by the Sea, by Yasuoka Shōtarō, tr. Kären Wigen Lewis 1984

Other Worlds: Arishima Takeo and the Bounds of Modern Japanese Fiction, by Paul Anderer 1984

Selected Poems of Sō Chōngju, tr. with introduction by David R. McCann 1989

The Sting of Life: Four Contemporary Japanese Novelists, by Van C. Gessel 1989

Stories of Osaka Life, by Oda Sakunosuke, tr. Burton Watson 1990

The Bodhisattva, or Samantabhadra, by Ishikawa Jun, tr. with introduction by William Jefferson Tyler 1990

The Travels of Lao Ts'an, by Liu T'ieh-yün, tr. Harold Shadick. Morningside ed. 1990

Three Plays by Kōbō Abe, tr. with introduction by Donald Keene 1993

The Columbia Anthology of Modern Chinese Literature, ed. Joseph S. M. Lau and Howard Goldblatt 1995; 2d ed. 2007

Modern Japanese Tanka, ed. and tr. Makoto Ueda 1996

Masaoka Shiki: Selected Poems, ed. and tr. Burton Watson 1997

Writing Women in Modern China: An Anthology of Women's Literature from the Early Twentieth Century, ed. and tr. Amy D. Dooling and Kristina M. Torgeson 1998

American Stories, by Nagai Kafū, tr. Mitsuko Iriye 2000

The Paper Door and Other Stories, by Shiga Naoya, tr. Lane Dunlop 2001

Grass for My Pillow, by Saiichi Maruya, tr. Dennis Keene 2002

For All My Walking: Free-Verse Haiku of Taneda Santōka, with Excerpts from His Diaries, tr. Burton Watson 2003

The Columbia Anthology of Modern Japanese Literature, vol. 1: *From Restoration to Occupation, 1868–1945*, ed. J. Thomas Rimer and Van C. Gessel 2005

The Columbia Anthology of Modern Japanese Literature, vol. 2: *From 1945 to the Present*, ed. J. Thomas Rimer and Van C. Gessel 2007

One Hundred Poets: One Poem Each: A Translation of the Ogura Hyakunin Isshu, tr. Peter McMillan 2008

STUDIES IN ASIAN CULTURE

The Ōnin War: History of Its Origins and Background, with a Selective Translation of the Chronicle of Ōnin, by H. Paul Varley 1967

Chinese Government in Ming Times: Seven Studies, ed. Charles O. Hucker 1969

The Actors' Analects (Yakusha Rongo), ed. and tr. Charles J. Dunn and Bungō Torigoe 1969

Self and Society in Ming Thought, by Wm. Theodore de Bary and the Conference on Ming Thought. Also in paperback ed. 1970

A History of Islamic Philosophy, by Majid Fakhry, 2d ed. 1983

Phantasies of a Love Thief: The Caurapañatcāśikā Attributed to Bilhaṇa, by Barbara Stoler Miller 1971

Iqbal: Poet-Philosopher of Pakistan, ed. Hafeez Malik 1971

The Golden Tradition: An Anthology of Urdu Poetry, ed. and tr. Ahmed Ali. Also in paperback ed. 1973

Conquerors and Confucians: Aspects of Political Change in Late Yüan China, by John W. Dardess 1973

The Unfolding of Neo-Confucianism, by Wm. Theodore de Bary and the Conference on Seventeenth-Century Chinese Thought. Also in paperback ed. 1975

To Acquire Wisdom: The Way of Wang Yang-ming, by Julia Ching 1976

Gods, Priests, and Warriors: The Bhṛgus of the Mahābhārata, by Robert P. Goldman 1977

Mei Yao-ch'en and the Development of Early Sung Poetry, by Jonathan Chaves 1976

The Legend of Semimaru, Blind Musician of Japan, by Susan Matisoff 1977

Sir Sayyid Ahmad Khan and Muslim Modernization in India and Pakistan, by Hafeez Malik 1980

The Khilafat Movement: Religious Symbolism and Political Mobilization in India, by Gail Minault 1982

The World of K'ung Shang-jen: A Man of Letters in Early Ch'ing China, by Richard Strassberg 1983

The Lotus Boat: The Origins of Chinese Tz'u Poetry in T'ang Popular Culture, by Marsha L. Wagner 1984

Expressions of Self in Chinese Literature, ed. Robert E. Hegel and Richard C. Hessney 1985

Songs for the Bride: Women's Voices and Wedding Rites of Rural India, by W. G. Archer; ed. Barbara Stoler Miller and Mildred Archer 1986

The Confucian Kingship in Korea: Yŏngjo and the Politics of Sagacity, by Ja-Hyun Kim Haboush 1988

COMPANIONS TO ASIAN STUDIES

Approaches to the Oriental Classics, ed. Wm. Theodore de Bary 1959

Early Chinese Literature, by Burton Watson. Also in paperback ed. 1962

Approaches to Asian Civilizations, ed. Wm. Theodore de Bary and Ainslie T. Embree 1964

The Classic Chinese Novel: A Critical Introduction, by C. T. Hsia. Also in paperback ed. 1968

Chinese Lyricism: Shih Poetry from the Second to the Twelfth Century, tr. Burton Watson. Also in paperback ed. 1971

A Syllabus of Indian Civilization, by Leonard A. Gordon and Barbara Stoler Miller 1971

Twentieth-Century Chinese Stories, ed. C. T. Hsia and Joseph S. M. Lau. Also in paperback ed. 1971

A Syllabus of Chinese Civilization, by J. Mason Gentzler, 2d ed. 1972

A Syllabus of Japanese Civilization, by H. Paul Varley, 2d ed. 1972

An Introduction to Chinese Civilization, ed. John Meskill, with the assistance of J. Mason Gentzler 1973

An Introduction to Japanese Civilization, ed. Arthur E. Tiedemann 1974

Ukifune: Love in the Tale of Genji, ed. Andrew Pekarik 1982

The Pleasures of Japanese Literature, by Donald Keene 1988

A Guide to Oriental Classics, ed. Wm. Theodore de Bary and Ainslie T. Embree; 3d edition ed. Amy Vladeck Heinrich, 2 vols. 1989

INTRODUCTION TO ASIAN CIVILIZATIONS

Wm. Theodore de Bary, General Editor

Sources of Japanese Tradition, 1958; paperback ed., 2 vols., 1964. 2d ed., vol. 1, 2001, compiled by Wm. Theodore de Bary, Donald Keene, George

Tanabe, and Paul Varley; vol. 2, 2005, compiled by Wm. Theodore de Bary, Carol Gluck, and Arthur E. Tiedemann; vol. 2, abridged, 2 pts., 2006, compiled by Wm. Theodore de Bary, Carol Gluck, and Arthur E. Tiedemann

Sources of Indian Tradition, 1958; paperback ed., 2 vols., 1964. 2d ed., 2 vols., 1988

Sources of Chinese Tradition, 1960, paperback ed., 2 vols., 1964. 2d ed., vol. 1, 1999, compiled by Wm. Theodore de Bary and Irene Bloom; vol. 2, 2000, compiled by Wm. Theodore de Bary and Richard Lufrano

Sources of Korean Tradition, 1997; 2 vols., vol. 1, 1997, compiled by Peter H. Lee and Wm. Theodore de Bary; vol. 2, 2001, compiled by Yŏngho Ch'oe, Peter H. Lee, and Wm. Theodore de Bary

NEO-CONFUCIAN STUDIES

Instructions for Practical Living and Other Neo-Confucian Writings by Wang Yang-ming, tr. Wing-tsit Chan 1963

Reflections on Things at Hand: The Neo-Confucian Anthology, comp. Chu Hsi and Lü Tsu-ch'ien, tr. Wing-tsit Chan 1967

Self and Society in Ming Thought, by Wm. Theodore de Bary and the Conference on Ming Thought. Also in paperback ed. 1970

The Unfolding of Neo-Confucianism, by Wm. Theodore de Bary and the Conference on Seventeenth-Century Chinese Thought. Also in paperback ed. 1975

Principle and Practicality: Essays in Neo-Confucianism and Practical Learning, ed. Wm. Theodore de Bary and Irene Bloom. Also in paperback ed. 1979

The Syncretic Religion of Lin Chao-en, by Judith A. Berling 1980

The Renewal of Buddhism in China: Chu-hung and the Late Ming Synthesis, by Chün-fang Yü 1981

Neo-Confucian Orthodoxy and the Learning of the Mind-and-Heart, by Wm. Theodore de Bary 1981

Yüan Thought: Chinese Thought and Religion Under the Mongols, ed. Hok-lam Chan and Wm. Theodore de Bary 1982

The Liberal Tradition in China, by Wm. Theodore de Bary 1983

The Development and Decline of Chinese Cosmology, by John B. Henderson 1984

The Rise of Neo-Confucianism in Korea, by Wm. Theodore de Bary and Ja-Hyun Kim Haboush 1985

Chiao Hung and the Restructuring of Neo-Confucianism in Late Ming, by Edward T. Ch'ien 1985

Neo-Confucian Terms Explained: Pei-hsi tʐu-i, by Ch'en Ch'un, ed. and tr. Wing-tsit Chan 1986

Knowledge Painfully Acquired: K'un-chih chi, by Lo Ch'in-shun, ed. and tr. Irene Bloom 1987

To Become a Sage: The Ten Diagrams on Sage Learning, by Yi T'oegye, ed. and tr. Michael C. Kalton 1988

The Message of the Mind in Neo-Confucian Thought, by Wm. Theodore de Bary 1989